My Memoirs

FROM TWO TO NINETY TWO

Betty S. Erickson

authorHOUSE®

AuthorHouse™
1663 Liberty Drive
Bloomington, IN 47403
www.authorhouse.com
Phone: 1 (800) 839-8640

Published by AuthorHouse   11/19/2015

ISBN: 978-1-5049-5896-7 (sc)
ISBN: 978-1-5049-5897-4 (e)

Library of Congress Control Number: 2015918121

Print information available on the last page.

Any people depicted in stock imagery provided by Thinkstock are models, and such images are being used for illustrative purposes only. Certain stock imagery © Thinkstock.

This book is printed on acid-free paper.

DEDICATED TO MY LATE HUSBAND
AND BEST FRIEND,

Richard B. Erickson

PREFACE

Hi kids, grands and greats, younger brothers, cousins, and all you in-law and out-law types. Just in case you think this will be a tell-all document . . . it isn't. This collection happens to be MY MEMOIRS and since it's MINE, I can write anything I choose to write providing it's the honest-to-God truth, as close as I can recall truth, and all from my point of view. So . . . if you've got your mind set on discovering closeted skeletons, the only ones you'll find are those I choose to let you find. So there.

Each chapter stands alone as a vignette; a scene I recall from the past. I believe that if the experience has remained in my memory all these years, it just might be interesting to readers. I'll start with my earliest memories and place them in chronological order as best I can.

I have never had a desire to track down ancestors and to brag or to admit I descended from them, so if you are looking for this in my memoirs. Sorry!

You won't want to read beyond this preface. BUT, if it's genealogy you want I can tell you where you can find it. My cousin Jacque, (Jacqueline Revis) in Salinas, California, has a treasure of knowledge and pictures that will tell you about our Grandma's side of the family. Jacqueline has no computer and no desire to learn how to use one no matter how hard I try to peak her interest. So, pack up your laptop and pay her a visit. She would be delighted to have you scan her pictures to your laptop and share with anyone who is interested. Jacqueline is a beautiful person both inside and out and she, unlike me, has great interest and knowledge of our ancestry much further back than grandparents.

Jacqueline Revis

My mother's maiden name was Erva Edna Lincoln and she was born on Halloween in 1899 in Calaway, Nebraska. Her family settled in Clearwater, California (now called Paramount) when she was ten years old. My maternal grandfather, Frank Allen Lincoln, was a school janitor, and my maternal grandmother, Linore Farrell Lincoln, boarded teachers. They invested wisely, owning four houses - two houses facing their other two houses on each side of Paramount Boulevard.

My mother was their only daughter. She graduated from Compton High School in Southern California. Before she married my father in 1921, she was employed as a secretary. I think her boss was a lawyer, but the only thing I know for sure about him is that he smoked cigars. Mother learned that good cigars "smell pretty good" but cheap cigars "smell really, really bad." Mother also taught children to play the piano.

My parents had two daughters, I was the first in October of 1923 and my sister, Joy Ann, came along in December of 1928. Our mother died of pneumonia in 1938, (before penicillin was available in Santa Cruz.)

My paternal grandmother, Margaret Douglas Couper (her peers called her Maggie, and Couper was changed to Cooper) was born in 1865 in Auchenlia Lanarkshire, Scotland, and she married James Monroe Young in New Mexico in 1888. They had four boys and three girls. My father, number six, was born in Jackson, Mississippi. in 1899. They named him John Cooper Henderson Douglas Young. I wish I had asked Grandma why she loaded my father with all those family names after naming the son one year older, Gay - without as much as a middle initial - just plain Gay Young. My paternal grandfather died when I was too young to get to know him, but Grandma Maggie Young became my beloved role model.

I don't know how old my father was when his parents moved from Mississippi to southern California, but he graduated from Gardena High School near Gardena, California. Gardena was an "agricultural" high school at that time, but its mission could have been to train students for any career that popped up. My father was curious and equipped with a lot of "good ole horse sense" and I wouldn't be surprised if his high school diploma were equal to, or even superior to diplomas from universities today.

My father was too young to enlist during World War 1 and too old to be drafted in World War II. His first "adult" job was driving a school bus in Taft, California, and at that time he was younger than some students on his bus. He had excelled in wrestling in high school and never let any training go to waste. When one of the older boys was acting inappropriately on his bus, he dealt with it promptly. He threw that kid off the bus, wrestled him to the ground and told him to walk home. Maybe that was proper punishment at that time, and maybe not. His bus driving career was brief.

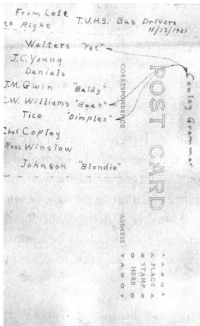

Next, my father went to work in the oil fields near Taft, California. I don't remember who told me this, but I suspect it's the truth. He informed his superiors how to perform a task in a better way once too often, so they canned him.

My Maternal Grandparents   My Parents in 1921

If you are looking for more genealogy, well . . . you can find tidbits imbedded in vignettes that follow. But your best bet is to fly our to Salinas, California, and talk with my cousin, Jacqueline Revis. I'll be happy to give you her address and phone number.

EARLY YEARS

ON BALDWIN STREET

AH - HA!

Here I am at Three Years Old

I'm thinking my way back through a bunch of decades to the time when I was no more than three years old. No one had warned me to be wary of strangers. Some strangers were interesting and some were not. Some spoke softly and some yelled. Some spoke to my parents and some were compulsive head patters. I hated that. Some strangers looked at me and smiled and my mouth wanted to smile right back at them. However, for a reason I can't possibly explain, I thought smiling at a person who was not a friend of mine was something I simply must not do. So, I stared back determined to muzzle my grin.

On a Sunday noon, my life changed forever. At last, the preacher was done and we walked out into the sunshine. I stood at the corner on Front Street in downtown Santa Cruz holding Mother's hand. Mother was talking to a member of our First Presbyterian Church and I knew her name was Ruth Hacking, but she was Mother's friend, not mine. When Ruth Hacking looked at me and smiled, I gave her my straight, steady look. She studied me a moment and then squatted down with her face so close to mine our noses nearly bumped, and she whispered,

"When somebody smiles at you, you are supposed to smile back at them."

Ah . . . . . ha!

An ear-splitting smile ripped across my face. Had an angel popped down to jiggle it loose? Do angels have wrinkled faces, names like Ruth Hacking and smell like coffee? Angel or no angel, my mouth was free to do what it always wanted to do. That was my first ah--ha moment! After that Sunday, the first thing people noticed about me was my whopping, big smile.

YOUNG'S WOODCRAFT SHOP

By the time I was two years old, my dad realized he had to be his own boss. He moved us from sweltering Taft to cool Santa Cruz by Monterey Bay and used his high school shop training and a heaping supply of good ole horse sense to set up his own business, Young's Woodcraft Shop, located on Front Street in Santa Cruz. He managed to serve satisfied customers even during The Great Depression years. I loved to visit his shop and breathe in the smells of newly cut wood and make trails through soft sawdust.

Mother liked to tell the story about a time she stopped by to visit Dad at work. A popular Hollywood character actress, Zazu Pitts, entered the shop carrying an antique accent table. Word was out that John Young's reproductions were good enough to confuse antique dealers and Zazu Pitts wanted a matching pair. Dad knelt to give the table a close look underneath, and his customer said, "I'm Zazu Pitts." Without looking up, Dad replied, "I'm John Young." He knew good and well who she was because he attended those ten cent movies regularly, but he didn't cotton to people who acted "high fallutin." Mother must have been delighted to see that actress close up because my mother did very good impersonations of Zazu Pitts and seeing her in person could have helped Mother hone her talent.

IN THE MIRROR

1930 Willys Knight

Grandmother and Granddaddy drove up from southern California in their shiny new Willis Knight. I turned four during their visit, and Grandmother decided to buy me a birthday dress. We went to Leask's Department Store in downtown Santa Cruz. I must have taken an exasperating amount of time to choose, because a dress from a place like Leask's was really special. Mother stood by patiently while I decided and undecided. Before Grandmother gave up and went to look at ladies' dresses, I heard her tell Mother she didn't know I was so particular and that I must have hated every dress she ever sent me. Mother assured her that everything she sent pleased me very much.

At last, I chose the perfect dress. Grandmother returned with a dress over her arm and said we would share a dressing room. I tried my dress on and knew right away it was a keeper. Then, I sat on a bench to watch while Grandmother took the new dress off the hanger, draped it over the back of a chair, pulled off the dress she was wearing, and stood there in her petticoat. Oh, how embarrassing! I'd never seen Grandmother's bare arms before. They were squishy, jiggly things that needed to be trapped in sleeves. I didn't want to look, and yet I couldn't stop looking. When she moved, they flapped. I watched Grandmother ease the dress over her head so as not to mess up her hair.

"Be a good girl and fasten the buttons," she said as she tugged to get the dress all the way down. So, I stood on the bench to do up the buttons and then watched while Grandmother tuned this way and that, viewing herself from all angles. I kept looking from Grandmother to her image in the mirror. I didn't want to believe that the scowl she wore in the mirror was also the scowl she wore in real life when she thought no one was looking. I had a scary glimpse of the real Grandmother Lincoln.

ALL THE STUFF WE
NEEDED TO KNOW

As soon as the big hand and the little hand got together on the nine, I gave Mother a hug, bounced out the door and barreled through a weedy lot where someone had tied up a goat. That was my shortcut to kindergarten. Bay View School's front entrance had a set of cement steps that appeared to me to be as wide and deep as those that go up to the Lincoln Monument. There was a wide, flat space at the top. Every morning all the kids except the eighth graders gathered on those steps. Eighth graders got to stand at the top. The start of the school day was one of the best parts. Miss Daglish, our music teacher, blew her pitch pipe and led us in songs like "A long, Long Trail of Winding", "Juanita", "Home on the Range", "My country 'tis of Thee", "Polly Wally Doodle", "America the Beautiful" and lots of others.

At nine o'clock, we stopped singing and two eighth grade boys went inside the building. One boy came out carrying the republic and placed it on the left side of the door and the other boy brought out the flag and carefully placed the flagpole in the hole in the republic. And then one of the big boys said, "Salute." We put our hands over our hearts and said, "I Pledge Allegiance to the flag of the United States of America."

The way we said the Pledge was different from now because Congress didn't put in those important words, "under God" until 1954. Another difference we had was Miss Lou Miles' idea. (She was our kindergarten teacher.) At the end of the Pledge, she told us to say, "We are Americans." Those words were so important to me that to this day I never say the Pledge of Allegiance without saying, "We are Americans" to myself at the end.

I felt proud of being an American even though several words in our Pledge were beyond my understanding. I thought that the Republic was that heavy chunk of lead with a hole in it where the eighth grader stuck the flag pole to make the flag stand by itself while we saluted it. After the Pledge, we sang, "Oh, Say Can You See," and we kept our hands over our hearts while those big boys carried the flag and the republic back inside. Then, we went to our own kindergarten building on the side of the playground and all the others went up the steps and inside the main building.

Our kindergarten room was big and bright with our colorful paintings and it had windows all around. Miss Lou arranged our tables in a circle with one table right smack in the center. Two of us sat at each table. Every day, Miss Lou picked one of us to sit at that special table in the middle, and the one she picked got to invite a friend to sit there with him or her. Sitting at that center table was a big deal because whoever sat there got to pass out graham crackers and milk and art supplies and they got to be line leaders at recess and going home times.

We sang songs and played games like The Farmer in the Dell and London Bridge is Falling Down. We did puzzles, stitchery, painting, drawing, modeling with clay. We cleaned up messes and put stuff away. We listened to a whole bunch of stories and we got to act out some of our favorites. Miss Lou didn't teach us to read or to write, but she showed us how to be friends and how to take turns and how to help each other. We had fun and learned a lot of good stuff in Miss Lou's kindergarten.

DID SHE OR DIDN'T SHE?

We sat on the curb outside our house on Baldwin Street in Santa Cruz, California, dressed in our best clothes and it wasn't even Sunday. Joidy, had celebrated her first birthday and I was her bossy six-year-old sister. We watched for Grandmother and Grandaddy to drive up from Southern California in their shiny blue Willis Knight. They always fussed over us like we were special.

Each time a car that was not blue or shiny rolled past, I pounded my fist on the sidewalk and Joidy did the same. When my fist turned red, I concocted a better plan. When a passing car did not bring our grandparents, I made my most disgusting face with my eyes scrunched up and my tongue thrust out as far as I could make it go. I even I stuck my thumbs in my ears and waggled my fingers. Joidy did the same. We had such a good time making terrible faces that I got careless and made a scary face when the shiny blue Willis Knight slowed and turned onto our driveway. Oh NO! We'd greeted Grandmother and Grandaddy with our worst ever faces!

Granddaddy parked and we ran to greet them. I hoped like crazy they had not noticed my terrible face. Grandmother picked Joidy up and carried her inside while I stayed outside to watch Granddaddy pull the cover over their car and fasten it down to keep it shiny.

Grandmother and Grandaddy brought us dolls. Mine had beautiful green eyes that clicked closed when I lay her down and popped open when I stood her up. I named her Alice. Joidy got a baby doll that cried when she squeezed her tummy.

Their visit came and went and Grandmother only patted my head and pinched my cheek. She never once picked me up. Maybe I'd grown too big for picking up but I wondered. Did she or didn't she notice my terrible face?

THE VERY NICE BOOTLEGGER

Mother sent me to Linstead's Market, our neighborhood store, to buy a pound of ground round. Mr. Linsteadt ground the meat, wrapped it in a neat package, and I gave him the coins I held in my hand. I wish I could remember the denomination of those coins. I know he gave some coins back. Mother cooked that ground round in a skillet on top of the stove with water, salt, pepper and pinches of flour to make the gravy thicker. Then she poured it over mashed potatoes. Since that menu and chipped beef over biscuits are menus I remember well, they might have been our steady Great Depression diet. Anyway, they were delicious.

When we heard the Ford pick-up rattle in the driveway, Mother put dinner on the table and I ran out to greet my dad while he stomped sawdust from his shoes.

Joidy, sat in her highchair aiming mashed potatoes at her mouth. Mother and Dad talked about bootleggers again at the dinner table, and on that evening, I listened. That very morning I'd met my first bootlegger. I had first-hand knowledge about these bootleggers grown-ups grumbled about but I was convinced they'd never even met a real one.

On Sunday evenings when aunts, uncles and cousins gathered at our Scottish Grandma's for "scones and tea," Mother, Dad and my aunts and uncles complained about bootleggers. My cousins and I paid little attention to grown-up talk, but we could tell they thought bootleggers were bad characters who were not to be trusted.

On that particular night, I was all ears. I knew my parents were good people but I also knew they were dead wrong about bootleggers. They didn't know a real bootlegger like I did so I had to straighten them out. I can't recall my exact words but whatever I said ended with, "My new friend at school is a bootlegger and she's very nice." That got their attention. I told them how my teacher had asked me to take some books to the library and I stumbled on the wide stairway and the books went flying. A bootlegger saw what happened and asked was I all right and I said I was. Then, she helped me pick up the books. She told me her name was Annie and she was in the sixth grade, and now she's my friend. I explained to Mother and Dad that bootleggers are not bad people and if they knew one like I did, they would like her.

Even though Joidy was squeezing mashed potatoes with both hands, I had our parents' attention. They wanted to know how I knew Annie was a bootlegger. I looked at her legs, of course. Annie had heavy metal boots on both legs and they made noise when she walked, but that didn't make her bad. She was my very good new friend.

I don't recall conversation after that, but knowing my father, he was probably impressed that his six-year-old had the gumption to defend underdogs. Annie was a polio victim who walked with support of braces on both legs.

FRECKLING IN THE SUN

It might not have happened had my dad been Italian, Portuguese, Chinese or maybe Dutch but he was proudly Scottish. Don't get me wrong. There was no finer person ever than my dad or my precious Scottish Grandma--the finest lady that ever stepped off the boat from Glasgow, she was. But all the Scotts I've ever known have attracted freckles like flies to a scone. I tried sun bonnets. That didn't work. I tried walking backward so Sun could beam me only from behind, but gave that up when people thought I was addlepated.

Then, one night I heard my dad say, "If you can't lick 'em, join 'em." Wow! What a clever idea! He was most likely talking politics but I applied, "If you can't lick 'em, join 'em" to freckling. All I needed to do was to let Sun pepper me with freckles, and then gaps between freckles would disappear and I'd sport a smooth, flawless tan. The next morning, I leaped into the skimpiest outfit I owned and challenged Sun to have a go at making me beautiful.

Well, Sun beamed away, penetrating me with enough risky rays to drive a dermatologist bonkers. At last, I recovered from sun stroke, bubbly blisters, peeling skin, and convinced my parents I'd sufficiently recouped my wits, but I still had that freckle problem. I tried powders and creams and scrubbed away, until at last. I got on to something.

I held my face down over a mug of hot cocoa almost close enough to touch the tip of my nose, and held that position until the cocoa stopped steaming. Then, I grabbed a mirror. My cheeks were pink and my freckles were definitely dimmer. Encouraged by this much improvement, I drank the cocoa, asked for more and lowered my face for a second time. When I lifted my rosy face from that second treatment and looked in the mirror, my freckles were gone! Problem solved! Yes! I'd saved myself and now I could save the entire freckled world. I danced on cloud 9 . . . for two whole minutes, and then I looked in that mirror.

THE BROKEN HOUSE
IN SCOTTS VALLEY

Grandma Maggie Young with my forever friend, Helen
Graham (Hall) wearing overalls and me in white pants.

When The Great Depression swallowed up Dad's woodcraft business in early 1931, his brothers were not doing well either. Dad had learned about farming as well as working with wood at Gardena High School. He drew up the plans and he and two older brothers built a large mushroom house in Scotts Valley, a rural area about five miles north of Santa Cruz. Then, they built a home my dad designed to accommodate a combination of families. And it did that beautifully. Since we approached that house from the back, that's the way I'll describe it - starting with the open side of of a wide, red cement patio - not red/red but a lovely pinkish/brown shade of smooth concrete.

On the far left was a bedroom for Uncle Whit and Aunt Lillian, a laundry room and a kitchen. Nearly always, we entered through the kitchen, a kitchen that had huge wood stove with a soup well in it. I don't think that soup well was ever empty because Grandma always cooked extra potatoes, meat and vegetables to resupply the soup well when preparing evening meals. Neighbor kids who were offered a bowl of soup after school thought that soup was delicious. As for me, I ate it dutifully as soup was served before every evening meal.

A spacious dining/living room stretched across the entire front of the house. A gigantic fireplace claimed a place between the living and dining areas. Instead of bricks under the huge mantle, Dad and my uncles selected granite rocks that glistened with formica and lit up like diamonds when fire burned in the grate or when sun graced them. Aunt Jeanette and Uncle Albert, missionaries in Thailand, came home on furlough every four years and brought back some lovely things. They furnished our living room with lamps and other accessories from Bangkok. The lamps were beautiful but the thing I liked best was a huge red banner that we hung above the mantle. It had dragons and other figures on it but the things that made it extra special were hundreds of tiny mirrors that were sewn into the fabric.

On the right side of the patio were three bedrooms and a bathroom that could be entered either from the patio or from inside. An outside stairway near the kitchen door led to my favorite place, a bedroom with a fireplace and a bathroom for Grandma.

On the right side of the patio, Mother and Dad claimed the bedroom near the living room and my sister and I claimed the middle bedroom and my teen-aged cousins, Harley and Douglas, the bedroom nearest the bathroom. Everybody moved in before that last bedroom was finished. It was lined with lathes that were left uncovered for several years because the men were busy and it didn't seem to bother Harley and Douglas that their room was unfinished. Because of the condition of that bedroom, my sister Joidy, who had just turned three, called that house, "the Broken House" and that name stuck.

Somewhere, my dad had found a huge stained glass window and they placed it above the long bathtub. The height of that window reached the ceiling. One who bathed in daylight was surrounded by rainbow colors and I know anyone bathing at night had privacy because I tried to peek in from the outside at night, and I couldn't see a thing.

Not far from the patio was a garage/workshop and my bachelor Uncle Gay had a private bedroom on top of that garage. I don't know whether he had a fireplace and a bathroom because the only way I could look in was by climbing a huge oak and looking through a skylight window in the roof and that window offered no more than a stingy glimpse.

Jupiter was Grandma's Great Dane. He was huge and looked scary to strangers but friendly and gentle with everyone - even little kids who tried to ride him when parents were not looking. When it was time for his dinner each evening he would stand by the kitchen door and bang his tail against the side of the house to remind Grandma it was time to feed him. Grandma cooked a huge portion of cornmeal and mixed it up with table scraps and served him this generous hot meal in a bucket.

A butcher drove to our house each week and Jupiter's LOUD bark got his immediate attention. To keep himself safe from Jupiter's jaws he tossed him hot dogs as he made his way to the kitchen and made sure he had enough left to get him back to his truck in one piece. Jupiter had a good thing going for him so we never told that butcher his loud bark was merely a greeting.

SCOTTS VALLEY SCHOOL

From the very first day, I loved that two-room country school. My cousin, Douglas, took me to the room with grades one through four and told Mrs. Blair that I was in the third grade. Then he went to his room on the other side of the hall with the big fifth through eighth graders. Douglas was in the eighth grade and Harley took a bus to Santa Cruz High School.

Mrs. Blair called each grade up to to a place near her desk to work with her one grade at a time while kids in the other three grades worked independently or helped or sought help from others. That classroom was never silent but I thought then, and I believe now, that it had just the right atmosphere for learning.

Recess was terrific. There was plenty of space for nearly anything we wanted to do - even a couple trees to climb. There was a little store next door to the playground. They had an outside counter where we could buy soup for lunch if we brought a nickel and they sold all kinds of penny candy. We could go there at recess time as well as lunch time if we chose to do so. Teachers expected us to take care of ourselves and I don't remember ever seeing a teacher on the playground. I spent most of my recess time upside down on monkey bars but sometimes we played a wild game with stick guns. Some of those guns were nearly two feet long and they had clothes pins at the end for triggers. Ammunition consisted of strong rubber bands made by cutting bands of rubber from inner tubes that were beyond use in tires. Girls' bare legs made great targets. Boys would capture girls by shooting at their legs, and once shot, a girl was taken to jail, a designated spot under a tree. I think the object of the game was to capture all the girls before teachers called us back inside. No one HAD to play the game, but that was my favorite and I had plenty of welts on my legs to show that I'd played.

It was on that very first day that I met Helen Graham, a spunky little first grader who became my forever friend. The Graham family had moved from Idaho and settled in Scotts Valley, California, to raise hogs. Hog business had failed because the land they purchased was a peat bog and hogs don't cotton to peat! But Helen's parents, like my own parents, had a knack for dealing with whatever life threw at them. There was a barn on their property and they had two cows and I think they sold milk but their main business was selling that peat. Mr. Graham put up a sign on the road in front of his driveway: J.J. Graham, the Peat Man. Helen and I walked home together that first day and every day after that until my family moved back to Santa Cruz.

THE CABIN ABOVE
THE CREEK

NOOOOOOO . . .

Since I wasn't involved in the work of moving, I bounced back and forth from beach to mountains content to put down roots wherever I was transplanted . . . except for one time. When we moved back to Santa Cruz and I was expected to transfer from my beloved two-room school in Scotts Valley. I sounded off so pitifully, Mrs. Owens, the principal and teacher of older kids at Scotts Valley, offered to drive me to Scotts Valley School along with her niece and nephew. That worked beautifully until our school picnic at the end of my fifth year when Mrs. Blair, confided to Mother that I would have more advantages if I attended Branciforte, the school in our district in Santa Cruz. It was nearly June of my year in sixth grade before I'd admit that Branciforte was "okay."

OUR COZY CABIN

When we first moved from our large family home in Scotts Valley to that cozy cabin, the cabin had no indoor plumbing except for the cold water that was piped into the kitchen sink and we had to go out our back door and down a path to get to the out-house. When Joidy and I bathed, Mother fetched the round tin tub that hung on a nail outside the cabin and put it on the kitchen floor. She heated bath water in a big kettle on the wood stove. I don't know how grown ups bathed but I know our parents could not have fit in that tub. After a few months, Dad added a part on the back of the house that included a shower and a toilet. I don't know how he got hot water for the shower and hot water to run through the faucet in the kitchen sink, but he could always find a way to do anything he believed was necessary.

The cabin had two rooms. Our parents slept in the kitchen and Joidy and I slept on a couch that opened up to make a bed in the living room. When we had company for dinner, our kitchen was crowded, so Dad cut a hole in the side of the cabin and extended the floor so they could push half of the bed through the opening to make more space. The half of the bed that stayed inside the kitchen made a good place to sit. Of course he put sides and a roof over the opening. He cut a small opening on the stove side of the kitchen and added a swinging door so Happy Luther Hooligan, our sturdy little Hines 57 terrier, could come and go as he pleased,

I think Dad moved us from the broken house because he wanted to be in business for himself. If his move caused a ruffling of feathers or breakdown in family relationships, it was so temporary that it went unnoticed by us kids. Our family remained "best friends" forever.

After we had moved back to Santa Cruz, Grandma invited my cousin Jacque and me to spend some summer vacation days with her. Grandma slept on a couch so Jacque and I could share her big bed and talk until at last we fell asleep. Along with my forever friend, Helen, we went swimming in a reservoir that someone, probably Helen's father, had fixed up with a diving board. Helen had no qualms about swimming and diving in that reservoir and I always had fun there but I only jumped from the diving board and never put my face in that water where frogs, polliwogs and most likely other critters lived. Helen went on to earn many impressive awards for her excellence in swimming and diving.

NO TRESSPASSING

On the other side of the road above our cabin was a wide compound with three large caves carved into the limestone bank. Those wide caves went deep into the bank, possibly 50 feet (but I write from a childhood memory and exaggeration comes naturally.) Each cave had a miniature railroad track, that extended all the way to the end. Those caves had been a winery before Prohibition and my parents converted them to places for growing mushrooms. They built 3-tiered wooden beds for mushrooms on each side of the track. Dad and Mother loaded the proper mixture of black topsoil and horse manure into large baskets they placed on a cart and pushed along the tracks. When the beds were ready they added the spawn to grow the mushrooms. Since mushrooms grow in the dark, Mother and Dad wore headbands with flashlights in them so they could see to pick those fast growing fungi. Mother wore boys' jeans when she worked in the caves because Levi and Strauss didn't make jeans for women. I wish I had a picture of her in jeans because I think you grandkids would have said she looked "hot." One cave was always "resting," so kids always had a cave with track and a cart to take turns riding and pushing and we had fun Halloween parties in whichever cave was dormant in October.

On the compound outside the caves, was a workshop where Dad stored wood and nails for building crates to ship mushrooms to sell to Levi and Zentler's Market in San Francisco. He showed me how to construct crates using a miter box he'd built to hold boards in place. I loved the smell of the new pine and the sound of banging nails. Pine was soft enough that I could sink a nail in one blow. My friends wanted to make crates too, so that was another plus about playing on our turf. And it happened that my wise Dad was getting free labor while keeping kids occupied. Why not?

In the winter, the stream below our cabin became a raging river. I wasn't aware of the danger at the time, but after we'd made our next move, I heard Mother tell Grandma that she was terrified when the water rose. Dad always hauled our little skiff, a tiny boat named H20-K9 (Waterdog,) up onto the compound when rising water threatened to sweep it away.

We took several trout from that creek and crawfish too. Helen and I caught crawfish by tying bacon onto a string. They'd grab the bacon and we'd pull them up to look at and then set them free. Some folks ate those things. Yuk.

Each year there was a time when steelheads swam upstream to spawn. It was illegal to catch them, but those were Great Depression years and those big steelheads were tempting. We'd hear them splashing their way upstream. I came home from school one afternoon just as my dad flipped a big steelhead out with a pitchfork and it lay flopping at his feet. Dad grinned and pointed to the NO TRESPASSING sign he'd nailed on a nearby tree. "Caught this one trespassing."

AMAZING GRACE

On the way to our First Presbyterian Church in Santa Cruz, Mother stopped to pick up my friend Grace Puget- not Pu-zhay, she was just plain Grace Pu-jet.

Sunday School followed by church swallowed an entire morning, stretching our sitting spans to the limit. Vibes from Grace were like quick little jabs to remind me we had an entire afternoon to explore. Yay, Grace!

Grace and I were the last ones to enter the partition where 6th grade girls met each Sunday morning. Miss Marsh sat with her hands folded across her Bible waiting for the clock's hands to reach 9:45. That place was spooky quiet. I don't remember if boys had separate classes or 6th grade boys simply didn't show up. As I think back on that situation, I know for sure that none of my sons would have gone back **willingly** a second time.

Miss Marsh bobbed her head up and down from girl to girl as she marked six members present on the attendance card. Then, she passed the collection basket, counted the money and recorded it on the attendance card as if such procedure were part of a high ritual. It's difficult for me to believe that six practically normal sixth grade girls sat in silence while this took place. But we did.

"Now, let us pray," Miss Marsh said in a voice that never rose more than one decibel above a whisper, and she reached for the hand of a girl on each side of her. We knew the routine. We held hands and recited the Lord's Prayer but did not say "Amen" at the end because there was more. Starting with the girl who held Miss Marsh's right hand, and you can believe I never put myself in that spot, each girl had to offer a prayer of her own. Miss Marsh did not allow silent prayers. I dreaded this. When I pray to God it is between Him and me and what I have to say to Him is not anyone else's business. My out-loud prayers in Miss Marsh's class depended on the weather. I thanked God for the sunny, rainy or windy day, whatever was happening outside.

When it was Grace's turn to pray out loud on this particular Sunday, it was like someone had popped the cork and words kept bubbling out. I knew Grace better than any of the others because she and I were in the same room at school and I nearly exploded trying to hold back giggles. She thanked God for the sparkling sunshine, the luscious green grass, the beautiful yellow flowers, the lovely purple flowers and especially for those little white flowers that look like bells but they don't jingle. Can you tell we were studying adjectives in our English class? Grace thanked Him for her honest parents, for her intelligent school teachers, for our dear Miss March and the President of the United States, the House of Representatives, the Senate and the Supreme Court. She thanked God for her dog, Licorice, and for helping the vet to make that ball Licorice swallowed come out of him without having to cut him open. Grace told God she was sure He hadn't forgotten but wanted to remind Him she was still waiting for a horse. She asked God to make her brothers nice to her all of the time, not just the times when someone was looking, and she asked Him if He'd mind giving her a new bike because her old one was a boy's bike and she needed a girl's bike . . . and on she went for more than ten minutes. Moments before giggles turned to hysterics, Miss Marsh held up her hand and whispered, "Amen." I don't remember whether or not there was time for the lesson.

After Sunday School was over we went to the sanctuary and sat with Mother in a pew near the center. Reverend Van Camp, the minister in 1934, ar-tic-u-la-ted each syllable so carefully his jaws must have been near collapse at the close of each sermon. The Reverend had a red-headed wife who moved about like she had ADDHD before ADDHD was invented and if their four year old son didn't grow up to be a demolition expert, he was ushered down the wrong career path. I don't think Reverend Van

Camp cared a whole lot for his flock and I doubt if his sermons warmed many hearts. When my Uncle Albert, a Presbyterian missionary, came home from Thailand on furlough, I overheard him say, "That man gives me a tummy ache," and Uncle Albert had a big tummy.

Reverend Van Camp's sermon on that particular Sunday could have been served up in five minutes but he concluded it as the clock struck twelve. Grace and I had removed pencils from the pew holder so we could doodle on our church bulletins. A few minutes into the sermon, I began tally marking each time the reverend ar-tic-u-la-ted the phrase: "God works in a mysterious way His wonders to perform." I noticed Grace was making exclamation marks, the fat kind that looked like baseball bats with balls on the bottom. Grace's vibes turned edgy and she pressed so hard she broke the lead in her pencil when the reverend let loose his (possibly twentieth), "God works in a mysterious way His wonders to perform." In a stage whisper that was heard across several pews, she said, "If he says that again I'll scream!"

Well, he did say it again and I braced for the scream, but Grace sat with eyes open wide and mouth zipped shut. People in front, behind and beside us craned their necks to look at Grace, and I'm convinced that some were disappointed. Mother pretended she didn't know us.

In case you want to know if we ever took Grace to church with us again, of course we did. Every church needs a Grace Puget.

BACK TO SCOTTS VALLEY

MUSHROOMS BECOME THINGS OF THE PAST

When I was in the 8th grade we moved back to Scotts Valley but not to the Broken House because it was once again occupied by other family members. Our home was on the road that led to Scotts Valley. We had an apple orchard and several cabins on the property. We found an old cider press in the tool shed and cleaned it up. We washed apples that had fallen to the ground, cut out worm holes and pressed apples to make delicious cider. At the edge of the property was a structure built for a produce stand where we sold apples we'd picked from the trees and cider that we had pressed. Dad purchased our first refrigerator, a General Electric with coils on top, so we could sell cold cider by the glass. That GE with coils on top hung in there for twenty years that I know of and possibly several years longer. In later years I learned that Mother and I made cider the hard way. Yes, you do wash the apples, but no, you don't cut out the worm holes. You simply boil the cider and the process of boiling and straining takes care of the elements people don't want in their drinks.

Dad no longer raised mushrooms. He'd shifted from growing and selling mushrooms to his two-truck trucking business. He loaded his aging trucks with the mixture of black top soil and horse manure that had been used for growing a crop of mushrooms and sold this "spent manure" to lettuce growers in Salinas. And then, possibly because he knew he couldn't coax his old Rio trucks to run much longer, he began selling insurance on the side. It didn't take long for Dad to realize that it would be more profitable to sell the actual real estate rather than the insurance on it. By the time he was 38, he had become a real estate agent.

Before I go on, I want to you to know that I speak of my friend, Helen, and other friends more often than I speak of my sister. My sister was a delightful person but I was five years older so she usually had her own friends or became a pesky little tag-along. It was not until I was an adult and she was practically grown that we realized what we were missing. Also, I left Santa Cruz when I was 17, so we saw little of each other after that - and that is one of my regrets. Mother named her, Joy Ann. When she began to talk, she called herself Joidy and that's what our family called her. Later she changed Joidy to Jody, and that became her business name: She owned and operated Jody's Pet Motel.

This is our family in 1937.
Left to right: Joidy, Betty Jean (me) Mother, Dad.

DODGING A MEETING OF MINDS

One evening decades later when I sat at the computer with two cats on my lap - creatures who could care less about the quality of my writing or the number of typos they caused, I planned to write about my most frightening experience. Well, I didn't actually plan to write about that topic. It was suggested by a member of a writing group I attended. Seemed like an easy topic. Right? Well, my fingers were poised above the qwerty keys ready to strike and the cats were at rest. It was time to get to work, but my fingers were not moving. What's wrong now? I groused quietly so as not to arouse the cats. I'm quite good at remembering, but I couldn't think of a single time when I felt really frightened. Good grief! I'd been over protected! But I have known when other people have been terrified.

The scene that came to mind was when Mother watched our dance performance. I was in junior high (now called middle school.) We were dancing for some club, possibly Kiwanis, and I was on the stage with my forever friend, Helen, and two of her brothers. Tom, was twelve like me, and Bill, my partner, was two years older. We were adagio dancing. When music teachers told me adagio meant slow, I was flabbergasted. Our adagio dancing was definitely not slow. Our dancing was much like what ice skaters do today - leaping and whirling and the boys catching us and tossing us around. At the end of our routine, Helen and I leaped to wrap our legs around our partners waists and we lay back while the boys whirled in place at great speed. When the dance was over, we took our bows and dashed off the stage. Mother, who was watching that dance couldn't speak for a few seconds. When she found her voice, it was no more than a whisper. She had wanted to scream, STOP! But she feared a slight change in timing could have caused our heads to crash together as we were whirled. Mother had been terrified!

At the time, I laughed. But thinking about it in later years gives me chills. What if that had been one of my children up there on the stage? Would I have had the good sense to remain silent? Or would I have called out and caused a meeting of the minds?

A BIG PENNY FOR MOTHER'S DAY

A bronze medallion has nestled in my jewelry box for more than three quarters of a century. When our children were small they examined the contents of that box from time to time and called that round chunk of bronze "the big penny." It's two and a half inches in diameter and weighs slightly less than four ounces. I chose a Mother's Day to write about that medallion. I had my mother for no more than fourteen years, but even then I was savvy enough to know I had the pick of the lot. She guided me through those early years gently but with such force I never forgot her teachings, sometimes spoken but more often by example.

The bronze medallion is an award presented by the American Legion to one boy and to one girl in a graduating class of eighth graders. Legionnaires meet with eighth grade students and staff to tell them what to look for in the boy and the girl they choose to receive these awards. Then students and teachers cast their votes. When I received that award, the traits voters were to consider were: courage, scholarship, service, character and companionship. Legionnaires still present this award but some of the traits they look for are different or worded differently. They still require the recipient to show courage, scholarship and service but the other traits are honor, leadership and patriotism. It's still called the "God and Country Award."

My parents were notified that I would be the recipient and they were invited to attend the presentation, but I never even dreamed that I might be chosen. Had it been a popularity contest, I would never have qualified. I was in shock when my name was called, but my legs walked me up on that stage and when I looked down and saw Mother in the audience smiling up at me, I felt as if I'd struck a grand slam, my Mother's Day gift to her.

MISS RICKEY

Miss Rickey aimed her Ford coupe down the mountain every Friday afternoon to dole out piano lessons at fifty cents a stop. By the time she'd worked her way down to our house, it was past dinner time and I believe her patience was spent. I put off torture for a half hour by insisting that my sister go first. I wonder why I did that. If I had it to do over, and I thank my stars, I don't, I'd go first and get it over with.

Miss Rickey began each lesson with those dreaded scales that I never played fast enough. She'd sigh and plant her hands on top of mine and push my fingers down on the keys. The minute she took over my hands, all I could think was, *Oh Lord get me out of here!* Those lessons occurred during the brief time in my life when I was a goody-goody. I practiced my pieces and I practiced those beastly scales. My sister practiced only when steered toward the piano dragging her feet. Even so I overheard Miss Rickey tell Mother she was pleased with her **younger** daughter's progress.

In May of 1937 Miss Rickey had a recital for her students. I don't remember what selection she chose for my recital piece, but it was so blah that Mother, who had been my first piano teacher, suggested I play "Meditations" instead. I loved that piece and Miss Rickey, praise the Lord, did not object. On recital night, Miss Rickey classified students in beginner, intermediate and advanced categories. I was in the intermediate group and members of the Santa Cruz Music Club judged our performances. After we'd all done our thing, judges placed the names of winners in three envelopes and presented them to Miss Rickey on stage. Miss Rickey opened the beginners' envelope, smiled, and read Donald's name. Next, she opened the intermediates' envelope, and gasped, "It can't be!" into the live mic, and then read my name. Later, she told me I'd "won the judges over" with my stage presence. I was "more poised than the others" because I was accustomed to dancing before audiences on that very stage. Although it pains me to admit it, she was probably right.

A LIFE CHANGING DAY

On a miserable day in July, 1938, lives were changed forever. As far as I could remember, the only time Mother had been ill was when I was five years old. On that occasion, she went to the hospital with a bad belly ache and came back a few days later, pain free, and presented me with my baby sister. Nine years later, Mother went back to that hospital and died of pneumonia before the day was over.

Grieving aunts and uncles with good intentions told me I must be brave. Aunts and Grandmother and Grandma could cry but I must not. I needed to stay strong for my father's sake. Somehow, I went through that funeral service without shedding a tear and so did my nine-year-old sister. I don't know whether she followed my example or they told her she must not cry.

I was a responsible fourteen-year-old sophomore and did my best to keep up with laundry, using a washboard in a laundry tub on our back porch. I packed lunches and cooked evening meals for Dad, Joidy and me.

1938 was the year San Francisco hosted the World's Fair. My first trip to the fair was on a Saturday with a group of kids from Santa Cruz High School. The driver simply parked the bus and told us what time that evening we were to return to that location. We were on our own to visit whatever we chose to see at the fair. My friend, Florence Phillips, and I went to a movie that showed the birth of a baby. That pretty much convinced me that having a baby was something I'd never do. I remember seeing many beautiful fountains and the lights on those fountains at night was spectacular. I don't remember anything about my next trip to the San

Francisco World's Fair except how I got there. Joidy and I rode in the back seat of Dad's car.

Even though our lives had changed, we still took those piano lessons. By the time my lesson was over Dad was home from work. Miss Rickey asked Dad if she could take my sister and me to the San Francisco World's Fair on Saturday. Dad agreed to let us go, and then she asked, "Would you like to go too?" When he said he'd like to go she said that they would need to take his car because we would be crowded in her coupe.

I don't remember when I stopped taking piano lessons. They simply fizzled out. However, the following summer, Miss Rickey married my dad, and she lasted forever.

THE DRIVING LESSON

A driver's license is something teens can't wait to possess. Right? Well, not all teens. Learning to drive was not on my to-do list. It was my Dad's decision. We'd been a father-daughter team for sixteen years, long enough for me to understand that he was an unshakable perfectionist. I learn by trial and error - many errors - many trials. When I WANT to learn something, I plunge right in making mistakes that I learn to fix one by one. Dad would study, observe, calculate, and then perform as well as, or better than those with experience.

I wasted a beautiful, summer day in Santa Cruz, California cowering behind the wheel of a Ford that had rolled out of a factory before I was born.

Dad told me to pull up the emergency brake. I could do that. He said I needed to set the brake to make sure the car would stay put while I learned about gears.

Those gear things were a puzzlement. If they had been marked, the marks had worn off. Dad said practice would give me the feel of those illusive gears and I would understand when, where and why I had to move them to drive the car. The thing that controlled the gears was a metal rod with a big knob on top that stuck up through the floor boards. I moved it up, down, sideways, and in the middle while I held down a thing called a clutch with my foot. When I'd practiced with those gears long enough to locate first, second, neutral and reverse, I thought the lesson was over, but it wasn't.

Dad said, "Now find the starter but don't step on it yet."

"What starter?" He showed me a bump of metal on the floor that occupied a spot that my toe struggled to reach. "Now you need to choke it,"

"Choke what?" I wanted to know. I could have choked about anything at that time. Dad pointed to a gadget on the dashboard that looked like a cigarette lighter and he told me to pull it out a little and push it back in to give the car some gas. That was something I could do. I gave it a hearty yank and then Dad told me I'd given the engine so much gas and I'd flooded it. I don't remember how he fixed the flooded engine, but he did and he was not happy. Never, ever have I heard my dad say a single bad word, but from the way the veins stuck out on his forehead, I think he needed to let loose a few damns to release the pressure.

Next, Dad told me to go ahead and step on the starter. The engine burped a couple times and then roared. I had one foot on the clutch and when Dad told me to release the emergency brake, I did. And then I slammed the other foot down on the brake pedal. The next move was to step on the gas pedal but I needed another foot to do that. I gulped and lifted the foot from the brake to the gas pedal and fished for first gear. Again, I lacked that necessary third foot -- and we were moving! The brake was the only part of the car that I thought I could control, so I yanked my foot off the clutch and slammed it down on the brake with my right foot on the accelerator.

What happened next convinced my dad that I was not ready for driving that day or any day soon. Never in the history of Fords has one leaped so high. When it came back down to earth, we got out unscathed physically, yet neither of us was ever quite the same. Three weeks later Dad got his old Ford running but he never said another word to me about driving, and you can be sure I didn't broach the subject.

GIRL TALK THAT NEVER
SHOULD HAVE HAPPENED

After Miss Rickey and Dad were married I called her Kathleen as I was told to do. Miss Rickey would never have been my choice for a piano teacher and she made it clear to me that I was not a talented student but I supposed she was okay as a person or even as my father's girlfriend. However, a short time after the wedding, she said something that killed any possibility of my acceptance of her as "Mom" as Joidy came to do. She told me that the first time she saw John (my dad) was when she gave her own piano recital. Her students and their families were urged to attend. She went on to say that she decided right then and there, that John Young was the man she was going to marry. That remark put a permanent knot in my stomach. Dad, **Mother,** Joidy and I attended that recital. From then on I never had time for "girl talk." I knew Kathleen did not kill my mother, but I felt like she had. I was not openly hostile, at least I didn't aim to be, but I was aloof, too busy with school work, youth activities at church. No time for any more girl talk.

Kathleen kept Dad from being lonely. We were getting over The Great Depression and Dad no longer had tough money problems. He and Kathleen made several interesting trips throughout the United States and Mexico and I was urged to go along but was in college and employed during the summer and simply not interested. Dad bragged that Kathleen was a wonderful travel companion who could always find interesting side trips and sights to see along the way.

Young Family of Six in 1944
Kathleen, Dad, Betty Jean, Frank, Johnny, Joy Ann

COLLEGE DAYS

MOVIN' ON

Dad and Kathleen presented me with a suitcase when I graduated from Santa Cruz High School. I tossed my clothes in that suitcase and they drove me to Stockton, two hours away. We went straight to the dean's office at College (now University) of the Pacific. Dean Beulah Lee Watson gave me a list of families who agreed to provide room and board in exchange for services from college students. They dropped me off at the first house on the list and two active preschoolers latched onto me. Their mother was happy to be freed from parenting each evening when the man-of-the-house arrived home from work. Responsibility for those two little boys plus my interest in big boys left little time for studies.

Fortunately, my modern dance instructor took an interest in me. Her health was failing and she had me take over the instruction of her modern dance class. I thought that was pretty cool especially since there were football players in that class. I suppose modern dancing was good for limbering up their muscles. Anyway, this dance instructor urged me to move to the home of her friend, Mrs. Weaver, who lived in a three-story mansion originally built for owners of the Sperry Flour Company. The grounds surrounding that mansion occupied most of a block and included a lovely in-ground swimming pool, a rare thing in 1941.

Mrs. Weaver had two children: Elsie, age twelve, and Peter, age sixteen. Peter attended Culver Military Academy in Indiana and came home for vacations and summers. The Weaver children were more like companions than responsibilities. My main job was cooking. I'd cooked meals at home, but nothing fancy. There, in that huge, well-equipped kitchen that included a butler's pantry, I learned to cook and serve elegant dinner parties in style. Mrs. Weaver's personal Fanny Farmer Cookbook pictured various cuts of meat that I'd never heard of and showed me how to make things like hollandaise sauce, something I'd never tasted. Mrs. Weaver taught me how to set the table in formal "Russian Style" and to serve properly using an array of plates and utensils, some I'd never seen before. She taught me how to form fancy butter curls to go on bread plates and to keep those elegant service plates in place until I placed a dinner plate before each guest. She outfitted me with grey and white striped everyday uniforms and deep maroon, lace-trimmed dress uniforms with fancy aprons. Besides cooking and staying with Elsie a few evenings when her mother went out, I received fifteen dollars a month. That was a big deal. Many of Mrs. Weaver's dinner guests were medical doctors whose daughters had gone off to college in style. Apparently college dorm food was either very good or full of calories, because most gained weight. I was the happy recipient of lovely hand-me-downs.

I ate my meals in the kitchen and appeared before guests and family promptly when Mrs. Weaver rang her little brass bell. Her son, Peter, hated to see me in a uniform. At that time Walt Disney's version of Pinocchio was playing in local theaters and Peter called me Cleo after that goldfish in the Pinocchio story. One summer evening, Peter, who was as tall and strong for his sixteen years as I was puny for my seventeen years bounded into the kitchen when I was serving dinner for guests, eyed my dress uniform with the fancy apron, grinned, and said, "Time you were back in the bowl, Cleo!" And he scooped me up, carried me out the back door and tossed me into the pool. That little brass bell was jingling when I sloshed into the kitchen. I barreled through the swinging door and into the dining room with my chin held high. Guests gasped and stared and Mrs. Weaver, usually soft spoken, bellowed, "Peter Weaver get yourself down here NOW."

While I slipped into a dry uniform, Peter removed the dinner dishes and guests had another round of drinks. By the time I appeared with coffee and dessert, they were in a jolly good mood.

THANKSGIVING TURKEYS

In the fall of 1942, I had my first turkey encounter. Fortunately for me, Peter was home on vacation from Culver Military Academy. Mrs. Weaver ordered two, large, fresh turkeys delivered from Gia DeLucia's Market. Those big birds must have been extra fresh because they were delivered with all their feathers still attached.

Peter and I accepted the challenge of "peeling those turkeys down to bare flesh without a pinfeather remaining. There was no Internet to instruct us as Al Gore hadn't created it yet and Fanny Farmer didn't tell us how to remove feathers, but we managed those things on our own. We used tweezers on pinfeathers. I can't recall cutting the birds open, so that must have been accomplished before delivery. I knew there was a thing inside called a gall bladder and if left inside it would spoil the turkey but neither Peter nor I knew what it looked like. So we cleaned out the insides of those turkeys keeping only organs we could identify - heart and liver. Once that was done, I could follow Fanny Farmer's instructions for stuffing and roasting a turkey, and since that kitchen boasted two ovens, that part was easy. According to Fanny Farmer, I needed to sew up the openings in order to keep stuffing inside those birds. The only sewing I had done was in junior high when girls had to make potholders and aprons. I preferred to keep things together with safety pins, so Peter located some really big safety pins, possibly the kind used to fasten diapers, and those pins did the job.

On Thanksgiving Day, I placed beautifully roasted, golden brown turkeys on silver trays with silver carving knives at each end of the long table. Not long after guests were seated, I heard laughing and jingling of that little

51

brass bell. Mrs. Weaver asked for an extra bread plate for the safely pins that Peter, grinning from ear to ear, deftly removed.

Just in case I left you wondering . . . YES! Those turkeys were delicious and so was the stuffing! Fanny Farmer and Peter gave me all the support I needed,

THE CHILDREN'S HOME
OF STOCKTON

At the end of my junior year, Mrs. Weaver sold that Sperry Avenue mansion and moved to San Francisco. My next move was to the Children's Home of Stockton. I had gone there with a story-telling group from college and fell in love with fifty precious children - all wards of the Court.

I'd already signed a contract to teach in the Stockton Unified School District in the fall but I'd graduate in May and had no plans for the summer. So, I asked Mrs. Ellsworth, the nurse in charge of Children's Home, if I could work there that summer. Immediately, she created a position for me as recreational director, a position I held through my senior year in college and for another two years after I became a teacher in the Stockton Unified School District. Life in The Children's Home of Stockton gave me the opportunity to get to know children of all ages - and I loved that experience.

Children at Children's Home were wards of the court because their parents messed up. Some parents stopped by for occasional visits, but I never once saw a tearful "goodbye." After a typical visit, the child dashed off to the playground and the parent sailed out the front door as if she had checked an item off her to-do list. I never witnessed a father's visit.

Matrons who worked at the home were like bossy grandmas who wore aprons with big pockets full of socks to mend. Ms. Atchinson was short and plump and could put on a stern face, but children knew which buttons to push to turn her into a marshmallow. She had a room near the girls' dormitory. She liked her coffee, and often had a coffee cup in one hand or at the other end of an ironing board. Barry, who was not yet four called it cowpee and that sent Ms. Atchinson into a tizzy. "it's not cow pee! It's coF- Fee," she stormed.

Mrs. Nichols' gout kept her from moving easily but she had eagle eyes. Her room was next to the boys' dormitory. The only time a boy got away with anything was when she made a conscious effort not to look - like when someone got a well aimed punch she believed he deserved.

The cook, Mrs. Ward, bustled in each morning to prepare breakfast and stayed until after our evening meal and older girls had cleared tables and washed the dishes. Children had their main meal at noon. Each evening, children had a light supper, often cereal or rice pudding and milk but Mrs. Ward prepared a regular dinner with meat. potatoes and vegetables for adults. At first, this difference disturbed me, but children never seemed to notice.

The Children's Home of Stockton
This picture shows The Children's Home of Stockton as I knew it in 1944. There have been many wonderful changes including new housing units for residents since that time. The structure pictured is now their museum but it was the only building that The Children's Home of Stockton claimed at the time I was there.

STINKY POTATOES

As I think back over my years at Children's Home I don't recall seeing sad children. No therapists hovered to make sure they had self esteem. Matrons urged me to don an apron filled with holey socks to mend while I watched children at play. But, Mrs. Ellsworth told me to join in their play and kick it up a notch. Lucky for those kids, she was boss. I never could get the hang of darning socks without making them pucker.

During my time at Children's Home, we had one child who came in at age two. We called her Wee Frances. Other children ranged in age from four to fourteen. I never heard any talk about age restrictions. Apparently, children came in whenever the court deemed it necessary.

Service organizations brought gifts for children at Christmas time and Masons came to take us to the circus. Sometimes individuals or organizations donated items and that's when I learned that generosity must have some restrictions. Someone, probably on Mrs. Ellsworth's day off, accepted a huge load of Idaho potatoes and stored them in the cellar. Mrs. Ward served them up baked, boiled, broiled, fried, in croquettes, curried, French fried, au Gratin, hashed, mashed, scalloped, souffléd, in pancakes, in soups, in salads and we used some for block prints in art projects - but summer days were hot and long enough to heat the coolest of cellars.

A horrendous smell wafted up from the cellar getting stronger by the hour until it found its way to the playground. When the Army drafted our gardener/handy-man, the older boys and I took over his job. I can't speak for the boys, but for me, hauling up dripping bags of rotten potatoes was the worst job I've ever tackled. We'd fill our lungs with air and plunge down into the cellar, grab leaking burlap bags of putrid potatoes, rush out of the cellar and dump that mess in garbage cans. To this day I can't think of any smell that compares in offensiveness to rotten potatoes.

My First Year as a Teacher

YES!

I knew from the get-go that I wanted to be a teacher and since I grew up speaking English, and I was pretty good at it, why not start with what I know and become a teacher of English language. However, when I observed the maiden ladies who taught English language in junior high and high school, I didn't think they they were having much fun. Also, the repetition was boring. The way I saw it, the difference between junior and senior high classes was no more than the maturity of the students. Curriculum stayed the same. Speech classes interested me more. Even though I quaked in my boots when it was my turn to speak, topics were unlimited. I could choose my own topic and learn interesting things while researching topics I chose. All I had to do was to hook listeners with a powerful opener, sprinkle in anecdotes to illustrate points, and then conclude my topic before the audience nodded off. I could do that, and I could help students to find ways to add pizzaz to their speeches.

I entered The College of the Pacific (now The University of the Pacific) in 1941 in the education department with a major in speech. Early that first semester speech classes were as exhilarating as I thought they'd be. But, college life had lost its spark by February. All it's get up and go had got up and went. Army and Navy had claimed most of the boys and all that remained was an overabundance of girls and a handful of 4F's (Army and Navy rejects) - a depressing situation for any girl with a minor in boys. Happily, spring arrived, and with spring came Commander Rokes and his Navy V-12 program to breathe life into our football team and perk up class participation and revive an assortment of extracurricular activities.

In my last year at Pacific, I did my first semester of practice teaching in a 6th grade classroom. Ed Esser, supervisor of elementary students in the Stockton Unified School District, came to observe. Immediately after that visit, he drove me down to the county building to sign a contract to teach 5th grade at Lottie Grunsky Elementary. Wow! He practically insisted that I sign a contract before I'd completed my education! I must really be hot stuff. (Actually, there was a critical teacher shortage.)

In September, when I met with 5th grade teachers at Lottie Grunsky, they informed me that the retired teacher I'd replaced had taught their music classes. In California at that time, special music teachers were not assigned to elementary schools. Classroom teachers were expected to provide music instruction for thirty minutes each day. A music supervisor conducted workshops, and if a teacher requested help, the supervisor would pop in to advise. Lottie Grunsky's 5th grade teachers informed me that I was expected to teach my own music and trade off spelling and a supervised study period to provide daily music instruction for the other two classroom teachers. I'd taken a music class for elementary teachers and I had a pitch pipe. What the heck! (I'd been conned.)

California had mid-year promotions at that time. When the second semester started, in came a bumper crop of brand new first graders, but there was no teacher and no classroom to put them in. No problem. Lottie Grunsky's new teacher (me) had done the second semester of her practice teaching in first grade. Administrators found a teacher to take my fifth grade and moved me to first and the auditorium became my classroom. Oh, what the heck! I could do that. I was young and invincible. Two months later, I was presented with a student teacher and I took him on without hesitation. Now, I shudder to think how little I had to offer.

After my third year at Lottie Grunsky, the county launched a pilot program for mentally retarded children and I was asked to work with the youngest group of mentally retarded children. I agreed to try it for one year. Since, I had no special ed certification, I enrolled in an extension course to learn something about working with retarded children. All I recall from instruction in that class is that I should never refer to children on my roster as mentally retarded. I should explain that I worked with CRMDs (Children with retarded mental developments.) That course was no help, but I gave those children my best shot for one year, as I had agreed. However, at the end of that year, my administrator refused to let me move back to a regular classroom. By that time I'd outgrown my "Oh what the heck" response. I resigned and moved to Alhambra, California, where I CHOSE to teach combinations of first and second graders and accepted student teachers from University of California at Los Angeles and Los Angeles State.

While teaching in California, I spent six of my summers at Mills College working with demonstration groups of 25 children ranging in age from five through seven. Children experimented with various art materials, worked with clay or wood to construct planes, cars and boats and some unidentifiable objects. They danced to recordings and drum rhythms, listened to stories, dramatized stories, swam, sang, hiked trails, explored ponds, and visited the campus bakery. They talked with the Chinese gardener who'd tended the vegetable garden as his father and grandfather had done; they visited a campus kitchen and experimented with body language to communicate with the Chinese cooks. The entire campus, a lovely country setting tucked away within the city of Oakland, was theirs to explore. And what a great way for me to get to know children!

Rather than to continue to pay rent during the summer while I was away at Mills, I chose to give up my rented apartment and find another place to live when I returned. Since I owned no furniture, I could fit my belongings in two suitcases and take them with me. Just before I left for Mills in the summer of 1950, I returned to my little garden apartment to find my landlady inside showing the apartment to a prospective renter - the most handsome and charming young man I'd ever met in my whole life. The apartment suited him perfectly and I told him I would be out of there in three days.

After much too short a time, the landlady and the tall, handsome man left and I was alone - but not for long. Five minutes later, there was a knock at my door.

"I'm back," he grinned. "Take you to dinner tomorrow night?"

"YES!"

WHEN AT FIRST I DIDN'T SUCCEED...

Well, this is one of those stories that has sulked like that nine hundred pound gorilla in the corner waiting to be exposed. I know kids can get just enough information to make them curious. Since I've been around longer than any other family member, my cousins' children ask me about things they either didn't or won't ask their parents or when they did ask, they didn't think they got straight answers. I suspect that's because they chose the wrong time to ask.

Out there somewhere, probably in that collection of pictures Jeff and Jackie are storing, there's a newspaper picture of me descending a spiral stairway in an elegant white statin bridal gown trimmed with pearls - a gown Mrs. Weaver's step daughter had worn.

The summer after I graduated from high school, I attended a Girl Reserve Camp in the Santa Cruz mountains as a counselor. There, I met Dottie and Franny Hull, from Stockton. Both girls were recent alumnae of the College of the Pacific where I would enter as a freshman the following fall. While at camp, Dottie and Franny, their parents, and their bachelor brother, Darrell, came to visit. When I arrived on the College of the Pacific campus, I was welcomed by the Hull family. Darrell, the eldest of the Hull siblings had been a baker like his father, but decided to attend the College of the Pacific and make a career change. In no time at all, he and I were steady daters encouraged by his family.

In 1943, fraternities lost many members to the draft each week and sorority sisters were frequent bride's maids or brides. Darrell was drafted and I became one of those brides. He was twelve years older than I, but what the heck! We were married and Private First Class Darrell Dean Hull was soon shipped off to New Caledonia, as a baker in the United States Army.

When classes started the following fall, Dr. McCall, my advisor, and one who had attended our summer wedding in Mrs. Weaver's home, introduced me by my new name to those in his speech class. I remember exactly what he said. "And here's Betty Hull who used to be Young (my maiden name) but she got married just for the Hull of it." That pretty much summed it up.

In 1945, the Army turned Darrell loose and he was once again a college student. By that time I was in my first year of teaching, a position I loved and was dedicated to. Darrell got weary of being "second fiddle to a bunch of first graders" and moved out. A couple years later, a stranger sauntered in to my classroom baring official papers for me to sign. I quickly signed papers. Darrell was suing me for divorce "on grounds of extreme physical and mental cruelty." Whatever. That chapter was ended.

Darrell was not a bad person. I was more attracted to his family than to him and in no way was I prepared for marriage. Last I heard of him he had remarried and was teaching in the physical education department at Modesto High School and he had two children. I hope he lived happily ever after.

So Kids, now you've heard it from the mare's mouth. I fell in love one time and one time only and that was with your father. I goofed up on the first go-round but got a second chance and that time landed the pick-of-the-lot. And you know that got you a super dad.

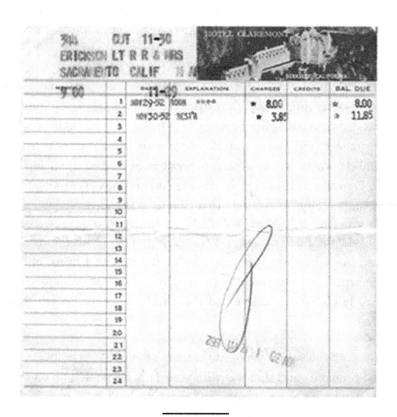

Our Wedding Bill

OH WHAT A RELIEF IT IS!

Public transportation served me well, but thirteen years later I found myself back in that driver's seat.

In 1952, two days after Thanksgiving, I persuaded Dick, the dude I found in my apartment who was now the handsome, intelligent Air Force officer I'd dated for nearly two years, to marry me. Before we moved to Ellsworth Air Force Base in South Dakota, we visited my family in Santa Cruz. Dick said I should learn to drive so we could share the driving on the way to South Dakota. His Pontiac had no gears or clutches to bother with. I had a learner's permit. I knew the rules of the road, and I knew how to brake and steer. And, most of all, I wanted to please my husband. After Dick drove out of the Bay Area traffic, I drove about seventy miles to Santa Cruz. The next day, he took me to the Santa Cruz DMV to get my driver's license.

I won't describe the behind-the-wheel part of the driver's test for fear of triggering a recurring nightmare. After the test, I pried my fingers off the steering wheel, stumbled inside the DMV and had my picture taken. Dick could tell he'd better not ask about my experience. We waited for someone to appear with or without my license. At last, the cop appeared, and he walked straight to Dick and handed him my driver's license with not so much as a glance in my direction. I can't recall his exact words but he ended with, "and she's in your hands."

A few months later, my sister, Joidy, called from Santa Cruz and told me she'd chatted with a person she hadn't seen since high school days, and he'd asked about her sister's health. Joidy told him I was fine, and then asked, "How do you know my sister?"

"We met at work," he explained, "and she gave me quite a ride! I gave her a driver's license on 99% hope and 01% ability."

I never liked to drive but I have a nearly perfect driving record (only one speeding ticket ever and that was at least 36 years ago). Last month, I gave up my car keys because Donn's car had succumbed to overuse, as he had racked up more than 300,000 miles in it. Now, when people at Westminster ask me to transport them to appointments or shopping, I can say, "Sorry, but I no longer have a car." Oh, what a relief it is. I stopped driving before I messed up my nearly perfect record.

RAPID CITY, SOUTH DAKOTA

TERRY

Our marriage was not Dick's first marriage either. His daughter, Terry, was nine years old when we married. Twice when we went for visits in California, she asked to come back to South Dakota with us. Each time she stayed long enough to attend a year in school. I well remember when she was in Milton Scandrett's 7th grade class and I went in for a conference on conference day. When I walked in for my conference, Mr. Scandrett jumped out from behind his desk and came to meet me saying, "You don't need to tell me who you are, because you look just like Terry." Rather than set him straight, I accepted the compliment.

It wasn't easy for Terry to have two homes, especially since they were a long distance apart. She had spent most of her life with her maternal grandparents and we understood that we should be satisfied with visits.

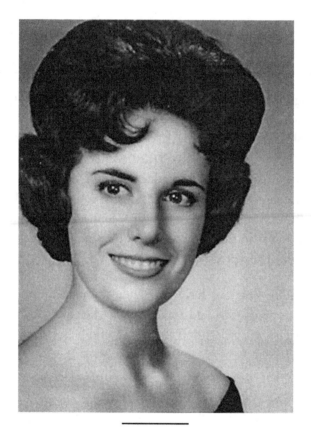

Terry's High School Graduation Picture
Doesn't she look like young Elizabeth Taylor?

IF I MUST WORRY . . .

When the alarm clock dinged in the dark of early morning, Dick silenced it before it threatened to blast us out of bed. "No need for you to get up - too early for breakfast."

Great! I pulled that one foot back under the covers and slept until the sun awakened Greg who was nearly three and Jeff, a toddler. Both appeared to be starving. As soon as breakfast was over and Terry climbed aboard the school bus, I lathered the boys with sunscreen and we headed for the playground. At that time,1956, we lived in a duplex in base housing at Ellsworth Air Force Base while builders put finishing touches on our home in Rapid City.

We hadn't been out long when I pointed to a B-36 flying overhead and told the boys, "Your daddy flies in a plane like that." At first, I thought I was watching a squadron of B-36's take off, destination unknown because the Cold War was dragging on. Soon, I realized I was not watching a squadron leave Ellsworth, but what I saw was a single B-36 circling the landing field and that B-36 was probably in trouble - burning off fuel before attempting to land. Was Dick in that plane? Nah. He left before daylight.

On our way home from the playground, we came upon three Air Force wives engaged in a conversation that stopped abruptly when we approached. They greeted me and made a fuss over Greg and Jeff. I didn't linger because my boys were hungry and tired.

After Greg and Jeff were fed and down for their naps, the concern that had been growing inside me began to take over. What were those women talking about, and why did they end their conversation abruptly when we showed up? Why didn't any of them say something about that plane? I tried to convince myself I had no reason to worry. Dick had left before daylight and this plane appeared several hours later. Those women had probably noticed I was pregnant again and were gossiping about it. They should mind their own business! Dick had to be all right. Don't look for trouble. Make yourself useful. Okay . . . Okay!

I hung a load of wash on the line, mopped a clean kitchen floor and vacuumed the carpets again. I was scrubbing finger prints off woodwork when the boys woke up so I furnished them with scrub rags. That was fun for about five minutes. but those little fellows sensed tension and behaved accordingly. Poor Terry, she must have felt like she came home from school to discover she was was living with two monsters and an obsessive cleaning lady.

Finally, it was bedtime for the boys and we put them to bed and Terry escaped to a friend's house. All was quiet. If that plane had crashed on the runway, I would have known about it, but Dick had not come home. The water in the bottom of the double boiler had burned dry but I didn't think his dinner had burned. I added more water and turned the burner as low as possible and stared at my spotless walls.

I was checking to see if the double boiler needed more water when the front door opened and a voice called, "Dinner ready?" I caught Dick in a hug that would have bruised an ordinary man!

The B36 crew discovered after they were airborne that their A-Frame was cracked and they had to burn off fuel before attempting to land. The landing had been uneventful. An officer returning from a different flight had come home sometime during the morning and told his wife that the plane Dick was navigating was in trouble. That must have been what those women were talking about when I approached. They didn't want me to worry about my husband being in that plane. If only one of them had come by to chat. If I must worry, I need a friend to do it with.

S-P-L-A-T

In the summer of 1957, when Greg was nearly four years old, and Jeff was two, and Mark was four months, Dick and his B-36 crew were temporarily assigned to Mather Air Force Base in Sacramento, California. The aging B-36's were being phased out and the crew was learning to fly the new B-52's. The trickiest part of that training was to learn to negotiate refueling in flight. Imagine how thrilling, or terrifying, that must be with two big planes connecting and disconnecting in flight. The shout, "Disconnect! Disconnect!" when the connection didn't go quite right rattled even the steadiest of nerves. It was scary enough to make some B-36 pilots change their minds as to what they wanted to do when they grew up.

This assignment to Mather Air Force Base was one of the few times our family could accompany Dick when he was assigned a temporary duty. We packed up our three little boys and left our home near Mt. Rushmore in South Dakota, and headed for the town of Atwater, California. Crew members with families spent that summer in three-bedroom housing units that circled a pool. Nice.

Since Dick and I both grew up in California, we were eager to return for a visit. My family lived in the Santa Cruz mountains, about a two hour drive from Atwater, and we drove there frequently on weekends. One Saturday, Dick stopped to fill the gas tank on the way to Santa Cruz. At that time, automobiles, at least those for ordinary people, were not equipped with seat belts and if there were things like special seats for toddlers and infants, they were unknown to me. After Dick filled the gas tank, he opened the rear door to rearrange things in the back and turned to say something to me. At that moment, Jeff, our two year old, had the sudden urge to jump into his daddy's arms, but his daddy had no inkling that such a precious catch was coming. Jeff went S-P-L-A-T, face down on the gravely turf. Jeff's face was scratched and bruised and he had a fat lip. We turned around and headed back to Atwater.

Jeff mended quickly, but Dick never fully recovered. He was sure he'd lost Jeff's trust forever even though the following weekend, our drive to Santa Cruz was uneventful and Jeff's injuries were barely visible.

Jeff doesn't think he remembers this early accident, but he's heard about it so many times, he isn't quite sure. But one thing he does know for certain is that his trust in his dad has never wavered.

Left to right: Greg holding Pamela Sue, Mark and Jeff

PAMELA SUE

On a crisp January, 21,1958 morning in Rapid City, South Dakota, our family consisted of a father, a mother and three healthy, and ACTIVE boys, all keepers no matter how much mayhem they stirred up.

That afternoon, our first girl arrived. The doctor dialed our telephone number, and then handed me the phone. Mrs. Boydson, the sitter who was doing everything but sit while watching our boys, answered.

"We have a baby girl!," I blurted, "and she weighs 14 pounds and 6 ounces!" I didn't understand why the doctor was laughing until Mrs. Boydson calmly corrected me. "I think you have those numbers reversed." Oops! But I got the girl part right.

Since I'd convinced myself we were not destined to have girls in our family, I had no girl-baby clothes, but that didn't bother me. Blue went perfectly with Pam's beautiful eyes . . . definitely her color. But neighbors thought differently and brought over an avalanche of clothes their girl-babies had outgrown.

I have always loved dolls and because I grew up during the Great Depression, I had only one, but that one was special. I named her Alice, because she was beautiful like Alice, one of my best kindergarten friends. She had big green eyes with thick lashes that opened when I stood her up and closed when I lay her down. Her long brown curls were like my friend, Alice's.

At last, with a daughter of my own, I had a perfectly good reason to buy dolls. However, Pam's interests were the same as her brothers. One

Christmas evening when Pam was nearly three, she came to me with a doll in each hand. "Mom, can you take care of these?" So much for dolls. I've bought dolls for granddaughters and now great granddaughters but I suspect they prefer stuffed animals.

I had known parents who finally got their girl or boy after several same sex siblings were born and they treated that last child as if he or she were more valued that the others. As a result, those children often acted like spoiled brats. I was determined not to do that to our beautiful Pamela Sue. For a time, I must have been way too hard on her but fortunately four-year-old Jeff brought this to my attention - not subtly but more like a stab in my chest. I don't remember what Jeff had said or done to Pam but I told him that was not the way to act. His response was. "You hate her and so do I." I was in shock for the rest of that day but got up the next morning determined to make known the love I felt for Pam to Jeff and most of all to Pam. Thank God I had sense enough to listen and to HEAR what Jeff was saying.

The summer before Pam entered kindergarten, she participated in a summer reading program for children at our local library. Just before school started, the library awarded some kind of prize to those who stayed with the reading program and read a certain number of books during summer vacation days. Pam had read enough books to qualify for that award but since she was not yet in school, there was no grade category for her so she didn't get a prize. She was furious and her brothers knew she had been wronged so we had our own award ceremony for Pam.

There was 14 months difference between Pam and Mark's ages and they became special buddies forever. When Mark inherited a bike from Jeff, (one that Jeff had probably inherited from Greg,) Mark was determined to learn to ride that two-wheeler on his own. He pushed it up and down hills and all around our neighborhood for at least a week, and then one day, he jumped on and rode it. When Mark thought it was time for Pam to learn to ride, he helped her onto the bike, gave her a shove, and off she went. She must have crashed on a lawn near the end of the street because she was not banged up. They came back radiant with Mark shouting, "Pam can ride a bike!"

I felt that I had done something right, no matter what message Pam's kindergarten teacher meant to convey. While in conference with that teacher, I said something about other children in the family and Pam's teacher was obviously surprised. "You mean Pamela is not an only child?" Thank you, Jeff.

CUSTOM MARY

When I look back on my life and and ponder mistakes I know I made, plus those other goofs I made without realizing it, I wonder how things would have turned out if I'd done more things right. I know there were times when I was unreasonable--much too strict, as well as times when when I should have jumped in as terminator, and didn't.

My response to WHY after I'd issued a "NO," was final. Discussion was over. If questioned further, I responded, "because it's customary."

Greg, our first born, understood that "because it's customary" made the NO final and he passed that knowledge on to siblings. I recall a day just before Greg was three, when he eyed me with soft, begging, puppy dog eyes, and then tuned away muttering, "I know, because of "Custom Mary."

The day our #2 son, Jeff, celebrated his 10th birthday, he asked, "Mom, why aren't you like a normal mom?"

"What keeps me from being a normal mom?" I asked, and Jeff explained. "Normal moms change NO to YES if their kids ask enough times, but you don't."

When #3 son, Mark, came along, it was natural for him to follow the Golden Rule, but I never had a chance to apply NO or my "because it's customary" on him because he didn't ask. Our yard and basement were equipped to interest, challenge and exercise young children, but Mark didn't stay put. His special friend, Mark Webb, lived across the street and down the block, and when our Mark got the urge to visit the Webb's Mark, off he went. Our street, East Idaho Street, in Rapid City, South Dakota, had little traffic, but any street is dangerous for a three-year-old to navigate alone. At regular intervals, I scanned the yard to check on children, and too often Mark was missing. I'm not sure whether Greg and Jeff didn't see him slip away or if they chose not to rat on him. I'd phone Mrs. Webb to ask if she had an extra Mark and "Yes," she did. My MA in Child Development with an endorsement in pre-kindergarten and nursery school didn't help me with Mark. I must have nodded off during lectures when instructors told how to keep a roaming pre-schooler in the yard without shackling him. I had to learn to deal with Mark from scratch.

Pam made her debut into the world when Mark was fourteen months old.

Mark could hardly wait until she became mobile. She became his special project and before she was a year old, he had her up and running.

Late one afternoon, Mark and Pam sat on the flagstone wall at the top of our front steps waiting for their dad to come home. Greg and Jeff had been playing catch and left a ball and glove there. Mark picked up the ball and was pounding it into the glove the way he'd seen the big boys do, when Dick drove up. Pam gave a squeal of delight and fell backward from the four foot wall. Quick as a blink, Mark flew off that wall in time to position that glove under Pam's head when she touched ground. They sprang back up and raced to embrace their awestruck dad. Neither Pam nor Mark remember that incident, but Dick never forgot and proudly referred to our Mark as Mickey Mantle Mark.

I smile every time I think about the morning when Greg and Jeff came up to breakfast with big grins splashed across their freckled faces.

"Okay, Guys, what's going on," I asked.

"We know who the . . . " Greg clapped his hand over Jeff's mouth.

"We know who the tooth fairy is, Mom, Jeff whispered. "It's you!"

They'd proved Greg's suspicion. Jeff's tooth had popped out the day before and Greg had sworn him to silence. They placed Jeff's tooth under his pillow without telling me, and when they woke up the next morning, the tooth was still there. Proof. No Tooth Fairy. Jeff stuck one hand out displaying the tooth and stuck a finger in his mouth to point out the hole. "Can I still have my dime?" he asked as best he could with his finger in his mouth.

I told him to find a dime on my desk.

As soon as Jeff had left the room, Greg confided that he knew about Custom Mary, too. "She's you, Mom, but I won't tell."

TODDLERS ON A SPREE

Mark and Pam, our numbers three and four children, have always been great buddies. Both were still living with us when they were nineteen and twenty. One night Pam was stuck by a drunken driver on her way home from work. She remained at Bethesda Naval Hospital for about two months. As a result of that accident, Pam received several thousand dollars- enough money to plunk down a deposit on a condo in Lake Ridge. When Pam moved to her condo, she asked Mark to move in with her. Later, when Pam married Dan, they both urged Mark to be a part of their family. And who wouldn't be glad to have Mark, a super mechanic as well as an outstanding person, in their household.

It's no secret that I'm pushing ninety three and, like many of my cronies, I think clearly in the past. So I'm going to show you a scene or two from when Mark and Pam were very young.

We lived on East Idaho Street in Rapid City, South Dakota, as I told you earlier. That was because Dick was stationed at Ellsworth Air Force Base nearby. Three-year-old Mark, knew the way to where his dad worked because we went there each week to shop for groceries at the base commissary.

One summer afternoon, Mark decided to go visit his dad. Naturally, he took Pam along. They walked more than a mile from our housing development and through a trailer park. Next, they would have been on the main highway to Ellsworth Air Force Base, but they were stopped by a woman (no doubt a grandmother) who spotted two and three-year-olds

81

walking unaccompanied toward the highway. She invited them in for cookies and lemonade, made a phone call, and chatted with them until police arrived.

Meanwhile, I, the negligent mother, had finally noticed they were missing. We had a spacious fenced-in backyard with sandbox, slide, swings, teeter totter and climbing apparatus. Mark and Pam had been in the yard with older brothers and a few neighbor children but none had noticed when they left. I was involved with housekeeping chores while toddler, Tim, and infant, Donn, were asleep. I could hear children at play and would look out the window from time to time but no alarming sounds came from the backyard, and I waited too long to take a head count.

Greg, Jeff, and neighbor children helped me search for Mark and Pam and we found no sign of them. No neighbors had seen them. I called their dad at Elllsworth Air Force Base. Then, I called the police. Before I could stammer my problem, the person on the phone at the police station stopped me. "Ma'am. What are their names?"

"Mark and Pam," I gasped.

"At this moment, they are in a squad car and Mark is helping the driver to find your house."

I hope I said "Thank you," but Dick's car was pulling into our driveway and I ran out to him. Before I could speak, we saw a squad car driving up our street. with Mark standing in the front seat waving his arms and pointing to our house.

Dick took over at that moment as he always did when we had big problems. While he fetched Mark and Pam and talked with the police, my wobbly legs took me inside to begin dinner preparation.

STILL STUCK IN THE PAST?

When a friend asked, "Was Grandmother Lincoln your maternal or paternal grandmother?" "Maternal," was all I needed to say, but my response was an avalanche of words. Few members of that little Paramount Presbyterian Church Grandmother attended would have recognized their stalwart member from my answer. She was the one they chose to take the collection plate home after Sunday services. She counted the money and deposited it in the bank the next day. She had a say in every move that elderly pastor made.

On a Sunday when we were visiting, Grandmother and Mother sang "In the Garden" at the morning service. Mother sang the alto part as it was written. Grandmother's soprano notes were stretched so thin I thought her vocal chords would snap. Composer Charles Austin Miles must have been doing flips in his grave. DON'T play IN THE GARDEN at my memorial service!

Grandmother was a superior cook. She boarded teachers who taught at Clearwater (renamed Paramount) Elementary School where Granddaddy was janitor. (Now, such workers are not called janitors; they are building engineers.) Grandmother's biscuits were always big, feathery light and piping hot. Her chicken and dumplings were pure ambrosia. Those teachers were so satisfied after Grandmother's dinners they never realized it wasn't a boarder's job to clear the table and help Granddaddy wash and dry the dishes. Once dinner was served and she was properly complimented, Grandmother's work in the kitchen was done. She sat by the radio darning socks, a job she claimed to despise even though she mended holes with a patch so flat and smooth it couldn't possibly stir up a blister. She was a perfectionist and that would have been fine with me if she hadn't tried so desperately to make me perfect.

By the time I was ten years old, I had stopped showing her my drawings, paintings, attempts at embroidery, and my new outfits. I stopped playing special piano pieces for her. I could never please her. She never failed to point out flaws and never seemed to notice the good stuff. In later years a psychology professor told me that was the way some people show they care. Try telling that to a ten-year-old.

However, Grandmother did possess a sense of humor and I kept proof of that for several years before I let it slip away. When I was in the second and third grades all the girls I knew had little diary-like booklets they asked people to write in. They may have been called autograph books. My cousin, Harley, was in high school at the time, and he autographed my book like this:

> "You are the best in all the West
> And I am better than you.
> But if you are good, once in a while,
> I will be thinking of you."

I asked Grandmother to write in my book. Before she wrote her piece, she read all the entries in the book, then wrote:

> "If you are the best in all the West,
> Someone deserves a lickin'
> For I'm the ma that gave your pa
> My one and only chicken."

After Mother's death, Grandmother came to stay with Dad, Joidy and me for part of that summer - about three weeks. I had graduated from ninth grade at Branciforte Junior High and Joidy was nine years old.

Grandmother supervised, while I scrubbed clothes in a tub on our back porch using a washboard and Fels Naphtha Soap. A clothes line stretched across our long porch. I had to redo hanging more than once, because unmentionables were in a place where they could be viewed from the road.

Grandmother drove me bonkers with "straightening up" areas in our house that I thought were perfectly straight, but she fed us well. She stayed with us for about three weeks before she got homesick for Granddaddy and her friends in Paramount. Also, she had teachers to board as school was about to start. She worried vociferously about leaving us. She didn't like the way I ironed Dad's shirts even though by then I'd had plenty of practice.

We didn't see Grandmother until a year later when my sister and I spent a week with her in Paramount when Dad and Miss Rickey went to Carson City to get married. I'd turned fifteen and Joidy, was ten at that time. Granddaddy always had a game up his sleeve and he had leveled off an impressive croquet court in their back yard. Grandmother cooked and baked scrumptious delights for us. Even so, I felt she had a not-so-hidden desire to get rid of us.

When a friend we called Aunt Grace dropped in, Aunt Grace innocently commented on how great it was to have grandchildren pay a visit. When she went on to say, "I wish my grandchildren were visiting with me," Grandmother's eyes lit up and she offered to lend Aunt Grace her grandchildren for two days and she would "come by to pick them up on Saturday." Well, Aunt Grace had two beautiful granddaughters of her own and Grandmother knew they lived near her, but she seized the opportunity to pawn us off.

Aunt Grace had a lovely little fish pond in her back yard. Joidy and I wiggled our fingers in the water and Jumbo, a HUGE goldfish, nibbled at our fingers. Jumbo was appealing but it was impossible to spend quality time with a goldfish for two days. We spent most of that time in the bedroom where we were assigned and came out for meals that would never have graced Grandmother's table.

I went on to finish high school and then graduate from College. After teaching four years in Stockton, California, I accepted a position in southern California that was no more than a brief train ride from Paramount. I spent a few weekends visiting with my grandparents. When Grandmother hosted a jewelry party, she invited my roommate and me. The party was fun and my roommate and I agreed to let the jewelry lady bring her party to our apartment. Since public school teachers were the only people we knew in Southern California at that time, we invited teachers and the principal from our building and the administrator who had encouraged me to move to Alhambra to teach. Grandmother accompanied that saleslady to our apartment. After the lady did her jewelry thing, Grandmother asked, and I suspect she knew the answer, "What do you do with the money you make giving these jewelry parties?" The woman answered promptly and much too loudly, "Oh, I use it for a very worthy cause. It pays for tuition to send my children to a private school," and went on to add, "public schools are such a disaster." That evening I added a new Thou shall not . . . to my personal commandments: <u>Thou shall not invite another saleslady into thy apartment.</u>

The next time I saw Grandmother for any length of time was in 1962 when she came to visit our family in Rapid City, South Dakota. We had six young children and the eldest was eight. Grandmother was eighty and recently widowed and we thought she would need her space, so we bought bunk beds to stack children in order to free up a private room for her. We told children not to enter Grandmother's room when her door was closed and five of six followed that rule. But Donn, who was not yet two, had learned to open doors. He opened Grandmother's door and in he went . . . much to her delight!

Donn has always brought out the best in people and Grandmother was no exception. Those two didn't use verbal communication in 1962 because Donn hadn't been around long enough to have acquired speech. Could it be that Grandmother took the time to know him as a charming little person because she was unable to tell him about his flaws? Or had she had changed through the years and was I still stuck in the past?

On the eve of the day I drove Grandmother to the airport, Donn spoke his first complete sentence. That evening, he told his dad, "Grandmother blasted off in her airplane."

EIGHT NATIVE SOUTH DAKOTANS

Uh-oh. I knew this day would end before I hauled myself out of bed. Dick was TDY (away on a temporary duty assignment). in Texas with his B-52 crew. It was only a 10 day assignment and he would be back in two more days. I was mildly irked because those ten days were in June. Why couldn't they have been in May or July?

The first order of the day was to call Mrs. Wright to make sure I had first dibs on the neighborhood sitter. She assured me she was available and would wait for my call.

Older children helped set the table, pour orange juice, fill cereal bowls and prepare toast lathered with apple butter. After breakfast, those on duty cleared the breakfast table and loaded our dishwasher, an appliance so new and wonderful that loading was a privilege rather than a chore.

After breakfast, our older kids, ages five, six, seven and nine, spread covers up to make their beds look presentable, brushed their teeth and came to check out with me before they went outside to enjoy a summer vacation day,

Before Dick left for Texas, he had mowed our lawn and then loaded the spreader with a fertilizer that was mostly nitrogen. That fertilizer grew our grass so lush that strangers driving by stopped to ask how we got it that way. The downside was that the grass grew much too fast. I'd already cut the stuff twice after Dick left and it was time for another harvest.

I plunked Tim and Donn, ages two and three, in a playpen, yanked the cord on the mower, cut the front lawn and dragged bags of grass to the curb. By the time I'd finished the front yard, the boys had tossed all the toys out of the playpen; Tim had climbed out, and Donn yelled in a language only Tim could understand.

I folded the playpen and we headed for the fenced-in back yard and got the boys interested in making roads for their cars in the sandbox.

By the time I'd mowed and hauled that last bag of grass to the curb, older kids were ready for lunch. We heated Campbell's Tomato Soup and made peanut butter and jelly sandwiches, doled out cookies and poured milk. After lunch the big kids cleaned up the kitchen and I put little ones down for a nap whether they wanted one or not. Then, I showered, checked the fridge to be sure tonight's dinner would be easy to locate, stuck two more notes with sitter's instructions on the fridge, and called Mrs. Wright.

"I'm on my way," Mrs. Wright answered, and she arrived promptly. We chatted briefly and I got my packed bag and climbed into the car. This was in 1962, one of the few years when military dependents could choose civilian doctors and hospitals. We had a brand new hospital on the other side of town but St. John's was on our side of town so I chose that old one. There was no hurry because my babies were never in a hurry. The Sisters took good care of me and called Dr. Bray who arrived in time to deliver Sara Jane.

The new hospital on the other side of town had a nursery full of babies, but St. John's Hospital's nursery boasted only two, our Sara Jane and one other. Since Sara Jane was our seventh baby, you can believe me when I say I've seen a few newborns but Sara never looked like a newborn. Her eyes were so big and dark I was sure they were brown even though they were hazel and she could track with those eyes from the start. And I swear she smiled at me that first day.

The only visitors allowed at St. John's were immediate family and no children under twelve. That meant no visitors for me but the Sisters popped in often and they they always had Sara Jane with them. That was really all the company I needed until Dick got home. But I began to worry. Did those Sisters ever put our baby down? I had not heard her cry other that one shout out to tell the world she'd arrived. Did she cry the minute they lay her down? Did I have a colicky baby? Oh no!

Dick flew in on the day Sara Jane turned two days old.

"Did you come to adopt the Erickson baby?" the Sister at the desk asked.

"I came to take my wife and baby home," Dick announced. "My wife is in room 204."

"Step this way," Sister said. And she brought Dick to me. Satisfied that he was the father, she sent someone to fetch our baby. Dick may have been annoyed when asked if he'd come to adopt the baby but when he told me about it, he chuckled. He was 41 years old at that time but his hair had thinned and he had grown a bald spot. He said that was because he had grown up through his hair. Since he was six feet three inches, that was not difficult to believe.

Our children approved of their new baby sister and took turns holding her. Sara Jane withstood the mauling without complaint and when we lay her in her bassinet that night, **that very first night at home**, she closed her eyes and didn't open them until the sun came up the next morning.

On the next page you will see Dick and me with seven of our South Dakota natives, Caris had not arrived yet.

Below, you see Dick and me with seven of our South Dakota natives, Caris had not arrived yet. Greg is standing in the back, Sara Jane on my lap, Pam on Dick's lap. Next is Jeff and then Mark in his typical pose with his hands in his pockets. On the floor you see Donn, (looking at his baby sister) and Tim is looking at the camera.

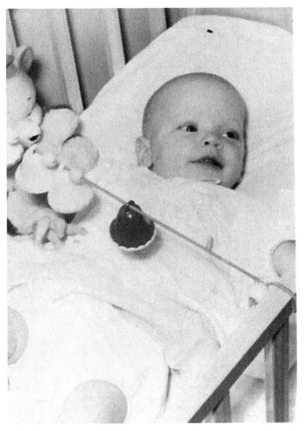

And here is Caris Anne, last but not least of our native South Dakotans. When we brought her home from the hospital, her siblings gathered 'round and burst into song when we told them her name was Caris. *Careless the Mexican Hairless* was the number one hit on the radio at that time. Even though she was a red-headed beauty, her siblings invited their friends in to view their Careless the Mexican Hairless and that song rang throughout our house. Even fourteen-month-old Sara Jane joined in on the fun. Even so, Caris was in no way damaged. She thrived on all the attention.

SURVIVING
BELLEVUE YEARS

GOODBYE, RAPID CITY, HELLO, BELLEVUE

In 1965 Dick was transferred to USAF headquarters at Offutt Air Force Base in Bellevue, Nebraska, where he was assigned to navigate on "Looking Glass," the airborne command post. "Looking Glass" carried on board the general who was designated to take over in a worse case scenario, that is, if the president, vice president and majority leader in the House were wiped out.

Dick stayed in a BOQ (Bachelors' Officers Quarters) until school was out and we would join him in a duplex in on-base housing. The morning after movers had packed us up, I loaded children in our Buick Invicta Station Wagon and attempted to join him. I say "attempted" because I'd never driven more than fifty miles from home. We arrived in Omaha just in time to be caught up in rush hour traffic and I couldn't find that elusive opening out of Omaha to get to Bellevue. Finally I gave up and pulled into a parking lot beside a telephone booth and called Dick. I told him we were in the parking lot by Caesar's (strip joint) in Omaha and if he wanted us, he would need to come and get us. He wanted us, thank Goodness, and he got a friend to drive him to that parking lot so he could drive us to our duplex in base housing. Whew!.

Lt. Col. Richard B. Erickson

MAY I SEE YOUR ID, MA'AM?

We enjoyed living in base housing at Offutt. That place even had two bathrooms! Donn entered kindergarten that year so we had one student in each grade at Fort Crook School, a five minute walk from our base housing on Billy Mitchell Road.

I liked everything about our duplex except the oven and stove. I was accustomed to electric appliances and there we had gas. The pilot kept going out and I'd called maintenance twice but they had other priorities. It took me so long to light that pilot that the flame would burn down to my fingers. I dropped the dying match and went off to do housework.

A short time later, I smelled smoke. Moments later, the kitchen was filled with smoke. I sent Sara and Caris to the neighbor in the other side of the duplex while I called the firemen. After making that call I went outside to join my little girls and the neighbor. The firetruck came quickly and the airman in charge said, "Ma'am I need to see your ID." I told him it was in the kitchen that was on fire and could he please put the fire out first.

It didn't take long to find the source of the fire and to put it out as it was smoldering in the drawer underneath the oven where the match had fallen. I had dampened and rolled up five or six of Dick's shirts in preparation for ironing and stashed them in that drawer. Those shirts were by no means easy to iron and manufacturers had already come out with no-iron shirts by that time. After the firemen had done their job, the one in charge copied something from my base ID and asked me if I'd like him to call my husband. I said, "No, thank you."

By that time several neighbors had gathered and they helped me celebrate my loss. (Ironing was never my favorite thing to do.) The kitchen cabinets including that drawer under the oven were metal and painted with yellow enamel. Fortunately the Base Exchange carried that exact shade of yellow enamel so I was able to do a super touch-up job before our next move.

STUBBORN WOMAN - GOOD NOSE

As the wife of an Air Force officer in SAC (Strategic Air Command,) I was accustomed to Dick being sent to remote areas for three month stretches of temporary duty. However, in 1967, Dick was transferred from SAC where he was navigator-bombardier on a B-52 to "Intelligence." He was given a thirteen-month assignment in South Korea at the United Nations Headquarters. The Pueblo Crisis took place while he was there on duty in Intelligence so I know first hand, Intelligence didn't screw up. The powers that be would not LISTEN.

Anyway, off to Korea, Dick went, leaving our eight children and me in Bellevue, Nebraska. We had to move off base (not because of the fire I'd started but because Dick was no longer stationed at Offutt.)

We'd lived in that area for a year before Dick went to South Korea, so I'd made some friends through Little League, school, and church, but I am not a bridge player and fitness centers were not the rage they are today, so I plunged headfirst into our children's activities. Our children ranged in age from two to twelve. Apparently, I overdid my involvement in our children's pursuits, because Greg, our eldest, came to me with a complaint and a suggestion: "Mom, you're messing in everything we do. Why don't you get a job?"

Hmmm. I mulled over Greg's suggestion that evening and in the morning called for an appointment with Mr. Cadwalleder, the person who hired teachers for Bellevue City Schools. He had a fifth grade position that needed to be filled yesterday as that teacher had put off maternity leave so long he feared fifth graders might witness a birthing. It was a snap to get a sitter for Sara and Caris, our two preschoolers. Mrs. Ellerbrook, across the street, had a small day care group in her home and I believed children under her care had proper supervision and were engaged in wholesome activities.

It was less difficult than I'd figured going back to work after a twelve year break. Each weekday evening, except Fridays, children helped with dinner preparation, clean up, and preparing lunches for the following day. On Friday evenings we all went to a restaurant. One Friday night after we'd returned from a restaurant, Greg asked, "Mom, what did we do wrong?"

Nothing wrong, Greg. Why do you ask?"

"The manager didn't come out to tell us how good we were."

Saturday morning, Greg took over like a sergeant in charge of a barracks while younger children vacuumed, scrubbed walls, dusted, and put away clothes. Our two little girls, Sara and Caris, "helped" me with the weekly shopping. I knew that Greg was pretty much a non-working foreman, but he got the job done and his workers didn't complain and bore no visible bruises.

There was a space of time, usually only one hour, but occasionally two, when our school-age children were home alone. I had one strict rule, and that was NO COMPANY WHEN MOM IS NOT HOME. At that time, and in that place, that was not considered bad parenting. Our little girls stayed with their caregiver until I went to get them.

One Monday afternoon, I smelled smoke as soon as I entered the house. Someone was burning trash down the street, but I thought the smell of smoke was stronger in the inside than the outside of the house. My nose kept leading me to a back bedroom.

While children were seated and eating spaghetti, I went back to that bedroom and used a broom handle to push up a covered opening in the ceiling that led to an attic crawl space. The smell of smoke was stronger up there. I called the fire department and told them that our house was NOT on fire, but I smelled smoke inside the house. They sent out one portly fireman who arrived at my door smoking a cigarette.

That fireman told me not to be concerned because the smoke I smelled was coming from down the street where a man was burning trash.

I asked him to please check the attic. He responded with a noisy sigh, stood on a chair and jiggled the cover over the attic opening, sniffed and came down.

"Ma'am, it's smoke from outside that you smell."

I insisted that he go up in the attic and take a look. He resisted, possibly he feared his mid section might not make it though the opening. However, to satisfy me, he mounted a chair on top of a chest, heaved himself up and squeezed through the opening into the attic.

"Hey lady," he called seconds later. Bring me a bucket of water and some rags!"

I rushed to fetch some old towels and filled a trash can with water and got it up to him. I heard him coughing and bumping around up there for several minutes. By the time he came down, he'd had an attitude adjustment. "There's a trail of matches and footprints that go from the attic in the garage to this bedroom," he announced. "Let me take a look at your kids and I'll tell you who was up there."

We went to the dining room where children were seated and he had them slide their toes back on the floor so he could see the soles of their shoes. Then, he walked around the table and stopped by our number two son, Jeff.'

Why were you burning matches in the attic?"

"So we could see where we were going."

"Who's WE?" I asked. A chorus of "Not me!" followed.

Jeff admitted that Dennis English had been with him, thus breaking the NO COMPANY WHEN MOM'S NOT HOME rule. At that point, the no longer reluctant fireman sucked in his tummy and talked seriously to Jeff and all the others about how close they'd come to real danger. "If your mother hadn't called for help, this house would have burst into flames about midnight. You'd better be thankful she's a stubborn woman with a good nose."

I sent this picture to Dick at Christmas time
when he was stationed in Korea.

NEVER WASTE KID POWER

Early one steamy Saturday morning, when Dick was in South Korea, I rushed from upstairs bedrooms carrying a mound of sheets I couldn't see over, burst through the living room headed for the laundry chute, and bumped smack into an object. I dropped the sheets, stood barefoot in my skimpy nightshirt growling, "What are you doing here?" The object I'd struck happened to be a neighbor who also happened to be our minister. He was taking his son to the lake to fish and had come to invite our older boys to go along.

That experience set me to thinking. Yes. I was definitely working too hard and losing my dignity as well. There had to be a better way. Kid power was being wasted. That was the last time I stripped a bed I didn't sleep in, or put away clothes I didn't plan to wear. I showed older children how to make those square corners on their own beds and told them to help little ones with theirs. Each child had a chest of drawers and a bit of closet space. I did the washing and ironing, but children had to get their own clothes from the laundry room and put them away. That system worked.

I was grateful to the home owners who risked renting to a temporarily single woman with eight children. They knew we would move as soon as school was out and I agreed to let realtors show the place to prospective buyers or renters from time to time, as long as they called before popping in. When a call would come, I'd tell Greg, who'd unleash a blast of tidying up orders for the downstairs, while little ones helped me make the upstairs presentable. That system worked.

Our two older boys, Greg and Jeff, ages 12 and 10, delivered the Omaha Tribune early each morning and and Mark and Pam, ages 9 and 8 delivered a local paper after school. Most of the time, children managed without my help, but when wind threatened to blow newspapers out of the wagon, or snow piled up, I drove the routes. Sleepy Bellevue neighborhoods looked quite different in the dark of five o'clock on a winter morning. Paper boys along with guardian dogs wheeled or trudged the streets ignoring skunks that were intent on finding a morning feast before the garbage trucks arrived. Skunks waddled down the street minding their own business ignored by savvy paper carriers and their wise dogs. That system worked.

*

In April, Dick came home from his 13 month tour in South Korea. He saw that we had a system that worked well enough that we were able to survive for a year without him. While he was pleased that we were in pretty good shape, I believe now that he was somewhat disappointed that we continued to thrive in spite of his absence. His next assignment took him to the Pentagon. Children and I stayed in Bellevue another month to finish out the school year. Dick occupied a space in the BOQ (Bachelor Officers' Quarters) at Fort Myers and spent considerable off-duty time with realtors looking for our Virginia home.

Not long after Dick had gone to the Pentagon, Greg asked me to take him to a gun show sponsored by Bellevue J. C.'s. I drove him and his friend, Arnold, to the gun show, and Arnold's father brought them home.

The next week, parent conferences kept me at school an extra hour. On Friday afternoon, I picked up Sara and Caris from their day care provider, drove inside our garage and entered through the kitchen door, calling, "We're home!"

"We're in here, Mom," Greg called from the quiet living room. I found Greg seated with three policemen. "What's going on here?" I asked but didn't really want to know. A policeman said there had been some trouble in our backyard and aimed his head at Greg who had discovered a book in the middle school library that explained how to build a pipe bomb. Well, that may not have been the author's purpose for writing the book but that was Greg's purpose for reading it. Greg and his friend, Arnold, had removed a leg from our outdoor grill and filled it with black gun powder they'd bought at the J.C. gun show. The explosion they created blew out six windows that faced our backyard. It also shattered one window in the house on each side of ours. Pieces of that flying metal grill leg imbedded themselves in Arnold's arm. Arnold needed help and Greg knew where to find it - only five minutes away via the shortcut. He marched Arnold down the hill to Bellevue's police station and got immediate attention. One squad car took Arnold to the emergency room and another transported Greg back to the scene of the explosion. I'm certain Greg was lectured on dangers of pipe bombs while they waited for me.

A neighbor on one side of our house was understandably irate. "Someone could have been badly hurt - even killed," he raged. A grandmother who lived with the family on the other side came out and asked what happened to her bedroom window. When told, she worried that she may have "gotten Greg in trouble" by asking that question.

Finally, the police left. Exhausted and numb, without a system for dealing with bombings, I telephoned Dick at Ft. Meyers. I don't remember how much I told him but I ended with "I can't handle this!" After a moment of silence, he responded, "I'll be right there." He didn't sound like the angry father of a kid who blew up a section of Bellevue, Nebraska. He sounded like a husband and father who was needed. I'm not sure how he managed it but he walked through our door that same night before the little ones went to bed. He must have caught a military flight that brought him directly from Ft. Meyers to Offutt Air Force Base.

The next day was Saturday. Greg and his dad repaired the neighbors' windows and all six of ours. Dick had a spring in his step and a grin on his face from knowing that there were flaws in our system that only he could fix. It took a bomb to remind me, but I never forgot that everyone needs to be needed and a family needs both parents on active duty to make systems work.

As for Greg, he didn't lose his desire to blow up things. He went on to get a degree in mining engineering and became project manager of the Red Dog Mine, above the Brooks Range in Alaska, a strip mine where they blow up rocks to extract lead and silver to get zinc that's used in automotive industries around the world.

THE FLIP SIDE OF PRAISE

While teaching in Bellevue, Nebraska, I was reminded of the time when Mr. Robinson moved from desk to desk while we worked at our seats. When he came to the desk in front of me, I heard him tell Robert Timius that he enjoyed meeting his mother at the parent meeting the previous night. He went on to tell Robert his mother is "such an interesting person." Next, he came to me and I expected him to say something about meeting my interesting mother. He didn't. He didn't even say he met her. Perhaps I would have forgotten that incident if my mother hadn't died a few months later.

Several years later I was blindsided by praise - this time the praise was for me. Principal Atwood at Birchcrest Elementary in Bellevue, Nebraska, where I taught fifth graders, was unpredictable and explosive. He terrified most students and teachers alike. He didn't rattle me that much, not because I was brave or tough, but because I knew I'd be leaving for Virginia as soon as the school year ended.

We used the Joplin Plan for language arts. That is, we divided children in our three fifth grades according to ability. I had the top two groups, cream-of-the-crop and high average. Since most of the readers in my groups were capable of working independently, I had the most students in my classroom at reading time.

At teacher evaluation time, Mr. Atwood visited my language arts lesson. That same afternoon we had a faculty meeting and he told faculty members he didn't want to hear another complaint about classroom size because that very afternoon he had watched Mrs. Erickson prove it is all a matter of organization. He went on to say that he watched a group of twelve work independently at a long table while Mrs. Erickson carried on a lively discussion with those in their seats. Midway through the discussion, four students returned from remedial reading, found their seats and went to work. He said he had counted forty four students in that classroom and they were all on task.

The kids at the long table usually talked among themselves and this didn't disturb me because at least some of the talk was about their work. However, with that particular visitor's eyes on them, they were silent. Normally, the remedial readers would have come to me for help, but they weren't about to call attention to themselves with Mr. Atwood watching. The discussion was particularly lively because only brave, confident kids who had something relevant to say contributed; I didn't attempt to engage any timid souls. As soon as Mr. Atwood left, one kid called out, "How'd we do, Mrs. E?" Then the kids replaced silence with sighs of relief, giggles and hi fives.

Even though I tried o brush Principal Atwood's praise off as undeserved, from that time on, the faculty regarded me as an obnoxious outsider, a military wife, who would be on the Birchcrest faculty just long enough to mess things up for the regulars.

EARLY DAYS IN VIRGINIA

TRAPPED

Nearly every weekend during that summer of '68 when we moved from the Midwest to Virginia, we visited a different famous landmark in our Capitol. One late Sunday afternoon, we paraded our eight children ranging from four to fourteen, into the Washington Monument. Unlike practice in later years, we didn't need to wait to get tickets and no one had cell phones to check. Dick and I kept little ones close as we entered an elevator and headed for the top.

At that time, visitors were allowed to climb the steps to the top. Mark, age 11, noticed the stairway and made a quick decision to scale those 897 steps. He got to the top, pushed on the door, but that door wouldn't budge. Since it was near closing time, a guard had locked the exit at the top of the steps and then began to usher the last groups of visitors into elevators. Mark, irked because he didn't get his view from the top, groused his way down those 897 steps in that hot stairwell and gave the door at the bottom an exasperated shove. He slammed his shoulder against it. He kicked it. That door wouldn't budge. He was trapped.

After admiring the view of Washington, D.C. from each vantage point, we herded little ones back into an elevator and rode down. When we reached the ground floor, we heard a commotion by the stairwell. A guard was yelling, "There's a kid in there!"

Greg, our fourteen year old, ran toward the guard shouting, "That's not just a kid. That's my brother!" The guard twisted his key in the lock and out came eleven-year-old Mark, red faced, panting, sweaty, and fighting tears because he was too big to cry.

On the way home, we stopped at a Burger King for our usual post-excursion treat and Mark refused a Whopper. Mark refused a Whopper! Only a death defying experience could curb Mark's appetite for such a delicacy.

The next day, with my encouragement, Mark wrote to First Lady, Ladybird Johnson, explaining how he had been trapped in the stairwell of the Washington Monument. Since Mrs. Johnson had taken on the project of beautifying D.C., he thought she should keep tourists safe and happy as well. A few weeks later, Mark received a form letter printed on official White House stationery thanking him for his "concern." We noted that it wasn't long after Mark's experience that visitors were no longer allowed to climb those stairs inside the Washington Monument. Of course Mark and I were sure we knew why.

Fortunately, our kids were resilient and I'm happy to report that Mark suffered no permanent damage, and I doubt very much if he ever refused another Whopper.

CONFESSION TIME

Dick, our hero, super dad, and my brilliant husband, promised that when he made his final military move we would at last get a family dog. Meantime, we had to be satisfied with ONE hamster and ONE canary.

Well, we didn't exactly follow that rule, and Dick understood my reason for breaking it. My own father lived too far away to be a the kind of grandfather who spoils his grandchildren properly. He and Kathleen raised basenjis (African barklless dogs) and my father was sure our kids needed a puppy. We agreed to accept a male basenji puppy named Boca.

As soon as puppies were weened, they were sold and unfortunately those sales included our Boca. Rather than disappoint our kids, Kathleen wrote that they had to sell little Boca but their grandpa would bring them a big puppy named Boca. So 2-year-old Katuro, became the big Boca.

But this big Boca, had been their stud and he turned out to be the only dog that neither Dick nor I were ever able to bond with. To be taken from his elevated position as stud and thrust into a family of children who wanted to play with him and love him and even called him by a name he never owned may have pushed him over the edge. He was too much for us - jumping our fence and chasing girl-dogs was an everyday occurrence. We had him neutered. Then he jumped the fence to get into garbage that was set out on collection days. He teamed up with a neighbor dog to attack garbage cans, by using his nose to pry up lids, then both dogs messed up our street and other streets as well.

I'd had enough. I hired a baby sitter, loaded Boca (Katuro) in the car and took him to the pound and had him put down. Since he ran off more than he stayed home, children didn't miss him and I didn't think it was important that I tell anyone I was the one who did away with him. Now you know, kids, and now that I have confessed. I'll get on with my Deacon Jones stories. The lesson I learned here was to stick to your dad's rules, *or else!* That particular four legged "or else" created havoc,

ENTER DEACON JONES

When Dick's last military assignment sent him to the Pentagon, Greg, our eldest, was a strapping fourteen. Our next two, Jeff and Mark, hadn't hit their growth spurts yet. Pam, our first daughter, either tagged after Mark or rode herd over younger brothers, Tim and Donn. Our youngest daughters, Sara and Caris, were sometimes mistaken for twins. Greg and Caris, our first and last, were true red-heads, but all had complexions that sizzled and speckled in the sun. As soon as they burst through the door of our "permanent" home, kids reminded their dad that the time had come to get that family dog.

Jeff would soon celebrate his thirteenth birthday, so he, egged on by big brother, Greg, concocted a way to insure getting that perfect pet. Jeff insisted that for his birthday there was one and ONLY ONE birthday gift that could possibly please him and that ONE gift was a dog—not just any dog but a <u>black</u>, <u>male</u>, <u>Labrador</u> <u>retriever</u>. Dick made it clear that if we should happen to locate such a critter, he would be a family pet—but Jeff knew that already. We searched ads in the Washington Star every evening, and at last found a breeder in Leesburg whose Labrador puppies would be weaned about the time Jeff turned thirteen. On July 16th, Jeff's birthday, Deacon Jones (named by the breeder after one of the greatest defensive football players ever) joined our family. In this next space I'll share a few vignettes about a period in our lives that occurred more than 40 years ago when our children and Deacon Jones were young.

At first, there was plenty of room for both Jeff and puppy Deacon Jones on the lower bunk, but Jeff took off on a growth spurt and Deacon grew into his huge paws. By the time Jeff had used up a day, he slept like a rock. When Deacon wanted to stretch out, he moved to the wall side of the bunk, planted his feet against the wall and pushed. Greg ceased to be surprised when he leaped down from his upper bunk to find Jeff asleep on the floor.

This is definitely a lousy poem but I never claimed to be a poet!

> July 16 in '69 is a day that's hard to beat
> 'Cus that's the day that Dad drove home
> With Deacon Jones in the passenger seat.
>
> We opened the door and out bounced Deacon
> With eyes shiny bright and tail a spinnin'
> All us kids were happily freakin'.
>
> Dad eyed Deak's paws and said.
> "With puppy paws as big as those
> He'll soon be big enough to pull a sled."
>
> We built a dog house for our pet.
> Encyclopedia Britannica showed us how
> 'Cuz Al Gore had yet to invent the Net.
>
> Deak's dog house was a work of art
> But Deacon never liked it
> He chose Jeff's bunk right from the start.
>
> But Jeff and Deak both grew fast
> As pups and teens are wont to do
> 'Til one morning, brother Greg stared aghast
>
> At Jeff on the floor and Deak in the bunk
> Deak had backed to Jeff and pushed the wall
> 'Til Jeff fell out - ker- plunk.

*

As soon as Deacon heard pans rattling in the kitchen, he'd bound upstairs, ready for breakfast. On Saturdays, boys often stayed in bed until their little sisters, Sara and Caris along with Deacon Jones came to torment them. The girls' first stop was the bedroom where the younger boys slept. That room sported a three-tiered stack of bunks they liked to mount to attack Mark up near the ceiling.

Deacon headed straight for Jeff and bopped him with his paw. Unfortunately, his claw hooked into Jeff's braces. Jeff yelled as best he could with Deacon's paw stuck in his mouth. Greg tried to separate the two, while the little girls ran for Dad, the solver of BIG problems. Once Dick took charge, the situation was more humorous than scary. Kids thought it was hysterically funny to see their brother with a dog's foot in his mouth and I tried hard to keep my composure. At last, Dick detached Deacon's claw and took Jeff to his grumbling orthodontist.

*

Donn, the youngest of our five sons inherited a few disadvantages, although he never complained. When time came to hand jeans down to Donn, a belt was absolutely indispensable. That belt had been brand new for Greg, but Jeff got it next, and he'd cut part of the end off and punched a new hole to fit his slim waist. Then came Mark, who'd punched another hole because he was the slimmest of all. Next came Tim, who'd needed more slack than Jeff or Mark's holes offered, but less than Greg's, so he'd punched in another hole. By the time that belt reached Donn, it was undeniably holey. On a Wednesday morning as Donn rushed to get dressed for fourth grade, the holes won. The belt fell apart. A less remarkable kid might have panicked, but not Donn. He headed straight for the box where he'd stashed Deacon Jones' outgrown collars and rummaged through the collection until he found the proper size.

Every Saturday, I had a mound of jeans to wash, and after washing unwashable objects from time to time, I'd learned to check pockets and belt loops before tossing items inside the machine. When I discovered Deacon's collar on Donn's jeans, I was overwhelmed with guilt. Only a no-good-very bad-terrible-mother would buy new collars for a dog while her precious son, her own flesh and blood, cinched up his pants with a hand-me-down dog collar.

Donn couldn't understand what all the fuss was about. After all, the collar was a good fit and it was practically new, having been handed down only once!

*

The community of Montclair has exploded with population during the past four decades, but when our kids and Deacon Jones were young, we were among the few who owned lake front property there. Lake Montclair is deep and wide and it winds around what is now an 18-hole golf course. We shared a private, sandy beach, with plenty of space where children could run or sprawl, and someone had secured a raft several feet from shore - just the right distance to swim to and to dive from. Deacon Jones loved to swim and he posed no problem for girls, but he must have either preferred boys or thought girls had enough gumption to care for themselves. For whatever reason, whenever our boys were in the water, he worried a LOT. As soon as they'd get in up to their waists, he'd rush to "save" them, and his saving meant painful claw scratches. The boys learned that anytime we had Deacon with us, it was best to stay on shore and watch their sisters swim.

One cool afternoon while we waited for the sun to ease out from behind clouds, Deacon spied a pair of beavers slapping their tails on the water and creating exciting ripples, and he swam out to investigate. Each time he started to close in on those beavers, they swam farther out. We worried that those tricky critters would tire Deacon - maybe even cause him to drown! We tried to call him back, but he was on a mission and ignored our calls. Finally, one of our sons came up with a sure-fire way to save their furry brother. Boys waded in up to their waists and yelled, "HELP!" Straight away, Deacon turned around and swam back. He had brothers to rescue.

*

Deacon was a short haired Lab but even so his winter coat grew in so thick that each summer he had bushels to shed. Fortunately, he liked being brushed and thankfully we had enough brushers so that one could take over when another tired. Deacon obeyed commands: Sit! Stand. Roll over. Lie down. At first, we bagged the hair and stuffed it in the trash, but when we noticed animated birds flying off with treasures of hair that missed the trash can, we let birds take over the recycling. Deacon Jones' generous contributions turned nests of local birds black.

However, in spite of frequent, vigorous brushing, Deacon deposited hairs throughout our house. I even found an occasional Deacon hair in the fridge!

*

One lazy Sunday afternoon, Caris was sprawled out full length on the floor of the family room. Tim, on cleaning duty, had given the old Hoover a quick swoosh through the bedroom he shared with Donn and Mark, and then powered down the hall as far into the family room as the cord could reach.

Suddenly, there was a CLUNK, followed by piercing screams that sent Dick and me racing downstairs. The Hoover had sucked up ends of Caris's hair, smacked into her head and was gobbling up long red strands when the motor stopped because it had more than it could handle. Once Caris knew Dad was in charge, her screams turned to whimpers.

"I need my tool box," Dick announced, and Tim scrambled to fetch it. Dick dismantled that Hoover spilling parts all over the floor. Then, patiently, he unwound those long red locks from the rollers and released Caris almost as good as new. I wanted to sweep up parts and stuff that hateful Hoover in the trash, but Dick put the beast back together and we used it until it succumbed to old age and I dumped it unceremoniously.

This is Deacon Jones in his mature years all decked out to ride in the passenger seat with one of his teen-age brothers at the wheel.

THE PANCAKE FLIPPER

It's not possible for me to look squarely at one of those gadgets cooks use to flip pancakes without smiling and that smile just might have a tinge of wickedness in it. For several years I had a pancake turner with a wide metal part attached to a metal handle. I think the handle was secured with rivets. Sometimes it swung from a hook in the kitchen where I could snatch it up it in an instant. Sometimes it was tucked in a drawer. But it was never misplaced. It was useful for flipping pancakes but that may not have been its primary purpose.

I know spanking is out of style now and it wasn't high on my list of things to do then, but I subscribe to the belief that a bit of force applied to a behind has great therapeutic value if done properly. My preferred method was to sit with the culprit bent over my lap, bottom side up. Then I'd draw back and swing at that posterior which was properly clothed, preferably with jeans. One good strike was sufficient and I don't think any of my strikes left a mark that would take more than a couple minutes to fade. After the strike, the matter was closed.

That pancake flipper moved with us from Rapid City, South Dakota, to Bellevue, Nebraska and finally to Woodbridge, Virginia. By the time it reached Virginia, Greg, our eldest, was fourteen, tall and strong like his father. One afternoon, he irked me to the point where I needed pancake flipper therapy. When I reached for the trusty disciplinary weapon, he bent over. I couldn't see his face but it must have had a grin on it because he was twice my size. I pulled back and took a swing at his buns of steel and the business end of the pancake flipper flew across the room. That last attempt at discipline with a kitchen utensil ended in laughter that will always ring in my ears.

PROBLEM SOLVED

Grandma Helen Margaret Healy (Erickson)
our kids paternal grandmother.

I walked in the kitchen with just one concern on my mind—what to fix for dinner. I thought about last night's conversation at the dinner table when we had liver and onions. Not a favorite with any of the kids but they knew the rules. If you don't like it, don't say so. Find something you like and go for it. It was okay to leave the offensive bit of food untouched. Grandma Erickson was living with us at that time and her doctor told her that the iron in liver was good for her blood. Deacon Jones, was eager for any leftovers.

The previous night's conversation at the dinner table had gone something like this. Why don't we have meatloaf anymore, Mom? Haven't had it for ages? Yeah. Yum. Why not, Mom?

Well, it would take about an hour to get a meatloaf on the table. I had some ground round thawed, so why not? While I busied myself with dinner preparation, voices from Caris, our youngest who was nearly six and Greg, our eldest, who was nearly sixteen, got louder. Greg, as usual, was taking over as man-of-the house when his dad was away on Air Force business. I perked up my ears.

"I did! I did! I did!" Caris yelled.

"No, you didn't. When you tell Deacon to 'sit' you've got to make sure he sits!"

"I tried. I pushed down on his behind like Dad said to do, but he wouldn't do it."

"You've got to show him who's boss. Tell him to sit and leave him standing and pretty soon he won't mind any of us."

I pushed the swinging door to enter the dining room where they argued. Deacon Jones was standing on his rug, that one place in the dining room where he was allowed to be, eyeing one and then the other with a Puckish look on his face - standing after being told to sit.

"What's the fuss about?" I asked, and Caris released crocodile tears.

"She told Deacon to sit and he didn't do it. So she just lets him stand there. She's got to stop ordering him around, or else make him mind when she tells him to do something."

I looked Greg square in the eye and asked, "Greg, what would you do if somebody told you to shit down?"

Greg simply cracked up. He'd never heard his mom say such a word.

Caris began to laugh even though she didn't know why she was laughing - probably relief that the tension was over.

That afternoon, I telephoned Mr. Laborwitz, a speech therapist, and explained that my daughter needed help with one sound she simply couldn't master. All s sounds were articulated as sh. After three Saturdays of speech therapy plus one extra for reinforcement, Caris had no trouble ordering Deacon Jones to sit.

ONCE UPON A BED

"Ye Gads! I'm drowning!" bellowed Dick from his side of our early-style waterbed. "I'm out of here!"

"I'm staying put," I muttered half asleep, and Dick leaped from the bed. An instant later, I was wide awake and screaming! I don't know what I screamed, but I know it was loud. Dick was six feet three and weighed twice as much as I, so when he ejected himself from his puddle, I rode up on the crest of a wave so obnoxious it flung me from the bed. I crashed against the wall and shivered in my soggy nightgown.

By the time I'd yanked off that gown and donned a dry one, Dick had a light on and his sense of humor had kicked in. He was laughing, but I wasn't ready to laugh. Not yet.

Dick located and fixed the source of the problem - a problem he had caused, by the way. He'd loosened the cap that sealed in the water with his long, prehensile toes. Fortunately, we had replaced our old Hoover with a Rainbow vacuum that could suck up water. Dick vacuumed water from the carpet while I fetched dry bedding.

In the wee hours of the morning, we climbed back into that contraption. So much water had escaped, our backsides bumped against the boards at the bottom of that box someone had the gall to sell as a bed.

After all that hullabaloo, we were wide awake . . . and that's where his tale ends.

TIM

Our #4 son, Tim, has always walked to the beat of his own drum. All our children loved animals, but Tim had a special knack for communicating with them. Had he been born in to a Catholic family, I'm sure St. Francis would have been his patron saint. When he was in high school he worked in a pet store that was near enough to our home that he could walk to work after school. I'm sure he knew every animal by name and loved them all but he was especially fond of Ralph, a silver Persian cat that was free to walk around in the store. He talked about Ralph a lot and I knew he wanted to buy him, but the cat must have been quite expensive and I didn't really understand how much that animal meant to him. A customer bought Ralph at a time Tim was not working in the shop. He was devastated when he learned that cat had been sold and when he learned who had purchased it, he was sure it wouldn't have proper care. I have always regretted that we didn't buy that cat for him.

One night while Tim and another boy were in the pet shop attending to animals, some rambunctious teens threw something through the shop door and the place was filled with smoke. I think Tim said it was a cherry bomb. Anyway he dashed home and got his older brothers who drove to the shop and loaded up caged animals and filled our family room with critters. The other boy also took animals home and I was grateful that he was the one who took the snakes. We had cats and dogs and a bird or two. The boys put all the animals back in the shop before they went to school the next morning.

I can't remember what Tim said, and whatever it was, he spoke quietly, but when Pam found an abandoned kitten and deftly maneuvered to get her positioned in the family without asking permission, Tim realized that asking was the wrong way to go about getting a pet. I don't know whether he thought his sister was really smart or whether he was angry, or perhaps a bit of both. Anyway, he loved Pam's Tigger and we were all pleased that Tigger welcomed puppy Deacon Jones and they became forever buddies.

At that time animals were free to wander about the neighborhood. When Tigger found herself in trouble with a dog or big Tom cat, she would head for Deacon, her protector. When Deacon and Tigger got too close to a mocking bird's nest they were both in trouble and would come home banging at the door for someone to let them in. Those angry birds dived down and pulled hairs from the top of Deacon's tail and from the back of Tigger's neck.

For a short time after Deacon and Tigger's happy lives had ended, we had no family dog, but we had a series of stray cats that decided our home was theirs. By that time Pam and our older boys had graduated Gar-Field High School and Greg and Jeff had moved out. One evening, Tim brought home a black Lab he named Banjo. He told me later that was how Pam got Tigger, so he wouldn't ask permission. To clinch the deal he brought Banjo home on his own birthday. That worked. We loved Banjo and accepted him as our family dog.

When Tim married and found work in Pennsylvania, he took Banjo with him. However, after a year, Tim realized the place where he lived was not a good place for Banjo, so he brought him back to us. Dick was delighted to have Banjo to walk again and Banjo spent the rest of his life with us.

One Saturday morning I left to attend an all day National Reading Conference. As I was leaving for Richmond, Dick and Banjo were headed for their morning walk on the power line in back of our house. When I returned that evening, Dick met me with no spring in his step and Banjo's collar in his hand. That told a sad story. Apparently, Banjo found some poison on that walk, became very sick and died before Dick could get him to the vet. That night I wrote to Tim and told him what happened. He called as soon as he read my letter. The first thing he said was, "Mom, how is Dad?" That was a typical response from Tim who understood that his dad and his dog had bonded.

CHANGED PREACHING HABITS

On a Friday afternoon while conferencing with a first year teacher about a first grader who came to me for extra support in reading, I mounted my soapbox and preached away without regard for the feelings of this "new" teacher. Her expectations for Cathy were so low I was convinced that she was not giving that child a fair shot at learning. As far as I could tell, this teacher saw no glimmer of hope that Cathy could ever achieve in school. I bristled and came on much too strong.

After that teacher had gone back to her classroom, I realized what I had done. I'd spoken like a know-it-all with 20+ years of experience and no regard for the person I was preaching at. I didn't listen. Thankfully, remorse kicked in before it was too late.

I marched myself down to that young teacher's classroom and found her sitting at her desk with tears in her eyes. I pulled up a chair and sat beside her and told her she shouldn't pay attention to old teachers who think they know everything. Then I reminded her about things she had done to help children achieve. When we parted I was the one with tears in my eyes and she was smiling. I'll always be thankful that God gave me insight to recognize this mistake and time to do something about it.

The next day was a Saturday and this young teacher invited a friend to her new home. The friend liked that home so much, she was interested in buying a house in that same development. Developers had set up a trailer where prospective buyers could view various floor plans they had to offer. While these two young women were viewing plans, a gunman came inside that trailer, forced the two women to lie face down and shot each one in the back of her head.

I still blunder though life making many mistakes along the way, but this experience changed my preaching habits forever.

POWER OF THE DANCE

Weather forecasters agreed that snow would start falling around midnight and continue throughout the next few days. Schools closed in neighboring counties but schools in Prince William County remained open. School busses loaded with grumbling kids passed by parked trucks loaded with sand and salt. Scowling teachers climbed out of warm beds and headed for school on a day they expected to sleep in. The sky hovered above like one huge dirty cloud. Temperature was snow-perfect and the smell of snow teased noses, but not one flake fell.

I switched on the lights in my third grade classroom and made sure I had lesson materials at the ready. I knew that most of my third graders would have stayed up late the night before as I had done, so sure we all were that schools would be closed the next day.

Before I let you in on what happened after the children arrived that day, I want to tell you about these particular third graders. Some had been with me since first grade and all those children who attended my first grade started out in the bottom quartile. The plan was for me to move on to second and third grades with children who were at risk of failure. Now, they call the process "looping" when a teacher moves to the next grade level with her children, but if they had a name for that in the early 70's, I never heard it. At the end of first grade, those who were no longer considered to be at risk were placed in regular second grade classrooms. The principal filled those empty seats with recently discovered "at risk" kids plus others who threatened to put the their teachers in St. Elizabeth

Hospital's psychiatric care. By the time my "loop" landed me in third grade I had eight children on my roster.

Before school opened that fall, the principal summoned me to his office and said, "Sit!" The tone of that command sounded like the one he used on Shorty, his dachshund. I remained standing.

"Sit. Please," he said. And I sat.

"You can't get away with having a handful of kids on your roster, so I've made some additions." He handed me an amended roster and said, "Now, take these third graders and I don't want to hear a squawk from you or any one of those kids or their parents all year."

I staggered out of that office with the saying, "Be careful what you pray for," ringing in my ears. Well, I hadn't prayed about this but I'd told that principal (who, incidentally, was my neighbor and very good friend) that he was harming those he put in my care by segregating them. I reminded him that every group needs some leaders--some good role models. No matter what this man said to me, I knew I had his support if I needed it. He was always fair with children, teachers and parents. He could call all 625 children in the school by name. However, he'd had the audacity to fill empty spaces on my roster with twelve kids based on their ability to create mayhem. Also, I knew that two of those parents, as he so delicately expressed it, "annoyed the crap" out of him.

Now, back to the day that should have been a "snow day" and wasn't. My third graders knew what they were supposed to be doing but they were not doing it. Some pressed their noses to the windows straining to spy a flake.

In desperation, I put a record in the record player. (No one had DVD players in the early 70's.) The record I chose was, 'Dance of the Sugarplum Fairies.' "Let's do a snow dance," I said, and the racket they made was deafening. I stopped the record player and explained that a snow dance only worked if dancers were silent - quiet like snow, took off my shoes and began dancing in my stocking feet. They took off their shoes and we danced together in absolute silence nearly to the end of that long record . . . when the sky split open and snow poured out.

While we waited for early dismissal busses to arrive, I tried to convince those third graders that our snow dance was simply a fun thing to do and it was a coincidence that snow fell when we danced. Some, possibly most, were not only convinced that our snow dance called down snow, but that our dance was powerful enough to close schools for more that a week.

LATER DAYS IN VIRGINIA

STRANGER THAN FICTION

At a faculty Christmas party at Springwoods Elementary School here in Lake Ridge, down the road a piece from Westminster, a troubadour waltzed in with three big colorful balloons, knelt by my chair and serenaded me. I was completely flabbergasted.

After the party I stuffed those balloons in my little Beetle and drove them home. I'd never driven such unruly passengers. They danced from front to back and banged against the windshield. Somehow I managed to get enough glimpses of the road to get us home. I wrapped the strings around my wrist, pulled them out of the car and coaxed them inside our front door. Once inside, they calmed down considerably and allowed me to take them down the hall to the den. When I let the strings go, they huddled together gently bumping the ceiling in the far corner.

In those days, Dick and I usually watched Wheel of Fortune and Jeopardy on TV after dinner. All of our children had gone off to homes of their own. One night while we were watching our programs, the balloons paraded out of the den and down the hall nodding and conversing with each other in balloon language. Josie and Winston, our two Labrador retrievers, scrambled to their feet and watched in awe as the balloons circled the living room and then went back down the hall continuing their quiet conversation as they reached their corner of the den.

This was not a one night performance. They appeared nightly on week days and always at that same time, but never on weekends. It would have been scary for me had I been home alone but Dick was with me so I knew

I was safe, even from evil balloons. Eventually, the dogs no longer stood to watch; they looked up and thumped their tales on the floor in greeting.

When pressed to think of a scientific explanation, we decided it had to have something to do with the air currants and/or temperature. On weekdays, Dick always bounced the heat up before I came home from school. Maybe that was it. Maybe not. On weekends, balloons stayed put. I can't remember how long that went on but I suppose it was until grandchildren claimed the balloons.

TOMMY AND THE NORTH WIND

Grandson, Tommy, tiptoed around the corner and inched inside the living room no more that three steps before racing back to the kitchen and grabbing me with so much force I nearly toppled. A few minutes later, off he'd go again. He'd creep around the corner and come barreling back. I learned to brace for the collision.

A wooden artifact on our living room wall both intrigued and frightened him. Since Tommy had yet to celebrate his second birthday, he didn't have words to describe how he felt but his actions told it all.

The woodcarving that bugged Tommy was sent to us by our eldest son, Greg, who made his home in Alaska. It's a rich brown/red color and heavy. I believe the wood is mahogany. The carving is about eighteen inches high and the width varies from nearly seventeen inches near the top to three inches at the bottom. The carving is an elder's face with deep set, old and wise eyes, a handsome long nose, sweeping mustache and a mouth drawn up as if to say, "Ooooooooooo" like the wind. His course hair fans out on each side of his head as if blown by polar wind and a wisp of misty cloud streaks though it. I named him North Wind.

When the family gathered in the living room, Tommy would prance in without hesitation. He'd play with a cousin, or wear out our aging pets, or dig for a toy that caught his interest, but every so often he'd take a sideways squint at North Wind as if he were thinking, You can't get me now, Mister, I'm safe . . . surrounded by big people.

A SPECIAL BONUS FROM WRITING CHILDREN'S BOOKS

I happened upon Seedling Publications, Inc. when I attended an International Reading Recovery Conference In Ohio and was browsing through book collections that vendors from children's book publishers had on display. I had written and attempted to illustrate stories for children in my reading/writing classes but until that moment at the conference, it hadn't dawned on me to submit a manuscript for publication.

Once I decide to do something, I go at it full steam. I zeroed in to Seedling Publications Inc. Their writers' guidelines read like they were written just for me . . . especially the line that stated, "We accept only child-tested manuscripts." I had a bunch of energetic testers eager to give a book a thumbs up or thumbs down and bursting to tell why.

In 1995, I submitted my first manuscript. A month later it came back rejected, but it was a "good" rejection. (The difference between a <u>good</u> rejection and a rejection is that a good rejection is <u>not</u> merely a form letter. It contains feedback from an editor.) I submitted two more and got two more good rejections. Then, I submitted <u>Oh, No, Sherman!</u> On a happy day in March of 1996, I received a postcard from a Seedling editor. All it said was, "Happy St. Patrick's Day, Betty!" The next day, that editor called and offered to send a contract.

Seedling books are a special category of picture books written for beginning readers. We read picture books <u>to</u> children not only for their enjoyment but to encourage language development. Beginning readers such as mine are written in children's language and pictures correlate closely with text to help beginning readers make sense of print with minimal assistance

Nearly every one of my sixteen published Seedling "readers" contains a part that is true although most are classified as fiction. <u>Oh, No, Sherman!</u> tells what happened one morning when our son, Donn, delivered papers with our family dog, Deacon Jones.

That same year, Seedling Publications published <u>Play Ball, Sherman,</u> a nearly accurate account of what occurred at grandson, Brad's soccer game. After those first two books came out, teachers requested a story about Sherman as a puppy. I never dared to dream that <u>Oh, No, Sherman!</u> would become a series of eight "little readers," but it did. Between Sherman submissions, Seedling Publications, Inc. accepted manuscripts on other topics. Fortunately, all my books are still in print and, yes, they have made me rich! - not rich in money, a better rich than that - friendship with Seedling editors Lynn Salem and Josie Stewart. Seedling Publications, Inc. was taken over by Continental Press but I gained two forever friends - a bonus that made me rich, indeed.

Here are some of my books for emergent readers.

MAGGIE AND JIGGS

This story is not mine but one your dad told and since he's not here to tell it, I'll try to do it justice.

When Dad was in junior high school (middle school) one of his jobs was to feed the reptiles in the San Diego Zoo. He lived on Arnold Street, a short bike ride from that zoo and it was handy for zoo keepers to have a dependable boy come in to feed the reptiles on days when the zoo was not open to the public.

At the age of thirteen, Dad was the proud holder of a key to the San Diego Zoo. The animals he looked forward to seeing the most were two huge orangutans, Maggie and Jiggs. Their trainer, an older gentleman, a retired or part time trainer, would enter the cage each evening after Maggie and Jiggs had their supper and sit at the table with the orangutans. He and Jiggs smoked their pipes. Maggie didn't smoke but looked on in good humor while the men indulged. Visitors often timed their zoo visit so they could watch this evening attraction.

One perfectly fine morning Maggie and Jiggs became restless and jumpy. By afternoon they stomped and banged at their bars as if they had gone mad. At three o'clock that afternoon they smashed their table and chairs and nearly tore the cage apart. Their behavior was such that your dad worried that even their trainer would not be able to calm them. The trainer never returned. He had a massive heart attack that morning and died at three o'clock that afternoon. Maggie and Jiggs were unconsolable and no one ever dared to enter their cage again.

THE FLIGHT SCHOOL RING

Your dad had a gold flight school ring with a brown jasper stone in it and that ring meant a lot to him. He was sad when it vanished from his finger. He searched in his truck and in our car and all over the house and yard and couldn't find it. He hoped to find it one day and never stopped looking.

About three years later, your dad found a huge pick axe just outside our back gate. It was a heavy tool, good for digging up very hard ground. He added it to his tool collection just in case he had need for it some day.

One cold, winter night several months later, Dad dreamed he was digging with that pick axe in the flower bed under our bay window and found his ring. Early the next morning, he bundled up and took that pick axe out under the bay window where a stubble of plants had been leveled by the cold. He swung that pick axe into the hard ground and was poised to strike again when he spotted his ring on the business end of that pick axe. He dropped the axe and dashed inside to wash his precious ring. It was as good as new.

A few hours later, your dad went back out to put the pick axe away, but it was gone and none of us ever saw that tool again. Whenever anyone noticed Dad's ring, a big smile would rip across his face and he'd tell the story of the pick axe that dropped by to help him find his flight school ring.

JOY ANN

When my sister, Joy Ann was learning to talk, she called herself Joidy and that is what my mother, father and I always called her. Most of her friends called her Jody and Jody Young became her business name. It was fun being her big sister when she was a toddler. The expressions she latched onto were priceless. When our dad wanted to reinforce a statement or a behavior, he would often conclude with "AND I DON'T MEAN MAYBE!" I can still visualize three-year-old Joidy reinforcing something she had said by stamping her foot and shouting "AND I DON'T MEAN IT TOO."

Later on when she was old enough to be a tag-along or get into my stuff, I was too busy brushing off that little pest to appreciate her. She had her friends and I had mine and we kept it that way.

**Joidy (Joy Ann Young) As I Remember Her
and the dog she's holding is a basenji.**

Joidy was fun-loving and bright, but ignored assignments in school unless she was convinced that what she was expected to learn would do her some good - like P.E. and art. By the time she was a teen, I had moved out. I knew she was an invaluable assistant to Doc, an aging vet, and Doc taught her well. Dad and Doc knew that Jody's high school grades would never get her in any school that turned out veterinarians. When Doc retired, Dad, with input from Doc and Joidy, constructed Jody's Pet Motel on a chunk of property that belonged to him and Kathleen. Jody had a ready-made clientele, as patrons already knew and trusted her from her years of working with Doc.

In Dad's late seventies, his heart began to fail and Kathleen, twelve years younger, cared for him until his death. After Dad died, I heard that Kathleen wanted Jody's business off the property. Jody owned the structure but not the property where Jody's Pet Motel was located. She felt she had to sue to get enough money to relocate, and she did. She bought a deserted pet care place in the Santa Cruz mountains and friends helped her make repairs, add dog runs, and move to that location that included attached living quarters. Again Jody's Pet Motel was in business. However, after suing, the story I heard (BUT I WAS NOT THERE) was that Frank, our half brother, his wife, Kathy, and Kathleen had nothing more to do with Joidy. who adored Frank's young children and was no longer allowed to see them. (**My facts may be screwed up here because I was in Virginia and saw none of this first hand.**)

In 1982, relentless rains flooded northern California and hit Santa Cruz hard. The rural area where Joidy lived was nestled among tall redwoods, and the soil became saturated. Joidy and others in the community sandbagged attempting to keep soil from slipping down the hillside.

On a dreary Monday afternoon, Jody stopped sandbagging and hiked down to her pet motel, possibly to feed the animals. While she was in that facility, an avalanche of mud uprooted redwood trees, crushed the residence part of Jody's Pet Motel and pushed its remains over the bank on the other side of the road. Jody was buried in that rubble and cadaver dogs found her body. two days later. Doctors said her death had come quickly and I pray they were correct. Most of Santa Cruz and the surrounding area was closed off. Dick and I flew from Virginia to San Jose to my cousin, Allen's, home and Allen and his wife, Fran, drove us to Santa Cruz for Jody's memorial service. After the service, Frank and his wife, Kathy, invited mourners to their home for a meal. I went along because I was a passenger in my cousin's car, but kept my distance from Frank, Kathy, and Kathleen. In my heart, I held them responsible for Joidy's death. If they hadn't forced her to move, she would not have been killed. But Dick, wise and thoughtful, knew we had only a piece of the story. He was gentle with me but did not shun Frank, Kathy and Kathleen.

It took ten years for my heart to thaw, and to get my head on straight but Dick was patient and eventually I came to grips with the fact that I never really knew what went on and that even if Frank had had been entirely wrong, (WHICH I NO LONGER BELIEVE COULD BE TRUE) I should, could and would forgive him. I opened up communication, and they welcomed me.

VISIT FROM FRANK AND KATHY

In 2001, Frank telephoned from California to say he and Kathy would visiting D.C. and surrounding area. Dick and I were pleased that they made our home their headquarters and we had a great visit. Frank and I talked comparing the dad he knew with the dad I knew. Dad was mine when he was young and feisty and Frank and Johnny got him after he had become older and mellow. Both "dads" were great people although quite different.

Frank and I attended Santa Cruz High School a generation apart. Alpheus Green had been my advisor throughout my high school years and Frank was in his advisory class and graduated the year Mr. Green retired.

Just before Frank and Kathy ended their visit, we hosted a family bash so they had a chance to meet nearly all of our family. Frank gave granddaughter, Sara Ashleigh, two disposable cameras and told her to "shoot away" making sure to capture everyone on film so he could take pictures back to to his mother (Kathleen.)

We never talked about those years I wasted, but every time we hugged, I felt certain Frank could feel my heart saying, *Thank you for forgiving me. I'm thankful I didn't lose you.*

MORE MELLOWING

I believe most people mellow with age. even though I've seen some turn brittle. Frank and I discussed the difference in the dad I knew with the dad he knew. Of course the times were different and that could account for some of the change. I had him during the Great Depression and Frank and Johnny, had him when he was not on Easy Street but headed toward that direction.

My conversation with Frank got me to thinking about changes in Dick and me. I remember the time when I picked up my first granddaughter, Miccah, at the sitters and we stopped at K-Mart on the way home. We hadn't been in the store more than five minutes when she darted from my side, ran over to a circular display of apparel, pushed clothes aside to clear a space and she used that space like a playground bar - jumped up on it and did her stuff. Had that been one of my children years before, I would have been mortified, but I was merely entertained by Miccah's antics. She didn't get hurt and she harmed no merchandise so what was there to fuss about?

Dick mellowed too. I remember the Saturday when he took 6 year-old Greg to the pediatrician at Ellsworth Air Force Base. While they waited to see the doctor, Dick looked down and saw a small hole in the knee of Greg's jeans and was so embarrassed he brought Greg home without seeing the doctor.

In later years we spent some time in the nursery getting plants to spruce up our yard for spring. After loading the plants in his truck, Dick asked if I'd like to go to lunch. He was wearing jeans and a shirt usually reserved for cutting the lawn but he'd mellowed to the point where his attitude was, "They'll love us as long as our money is green."

WINSTON

I had a beloved friend named Winston. We were kindred spirits and I think he knew me better than any of my other friends. We'd been through many happy times together and a few tragedies as well. Even in the midst of a really difficult time, he let me know that there were still many good times ahead. I could talk with Winston about anything and know that my secret was safe with him.

Winston was jet black, walked on four sturdy legs and when I looked into his dark brown eyes, pure love shone back at me. There were times when I buried my face in his fur and wept, but it never occurred to him to call me a wimp.

Winston was playful and his collection of toys were important to him. I rarely went shopping without bringing home some kind of a doggie toy that would make a sound if pressed in a certain spot. Squeaker toys were his favorites.

Winston was a great entertainer and he put on special shows for just for me. He'd gather a bunch of his squeaker toys and place them in a semi circle in front of him. Then, he'd pick up one toy at a time, shake it or bite it gently to release its sound. And then he'd put that toy down and pick up the next bringing smiles and claps from his private audience.

Winston shared his responsibility as host. He'd rush to find a present for the visitor and if the visitor was new to his ways, Winston would nudge that visitor with his gift until he accepted it or I had to intervene. He was generous with his love but not with his toys. The presents he chose to give visitors never came from his musical collection. Items on my coffee table were usually his first choice. Things like newspapers, books or magazines but sometimes he'd go into my bedroom and grab a slipper or an item from my dresser. One morning he brought a visitor my bra and that caused so much laughter that I had to be very careful to have my bras safe in a closed drawer. He was definitely pleased with the reaction the gift of my bra made and was eager to do an encore.

One evening, a few days after Dick's death, I'd been watching the news on television and noticed the room was chilly. I walked over to the thermostat and stood there looking at it and feeling uneasy about turning that dial. Winston made a strange sound that seemed to come from the back of his throat. When I turned that dial up a notch, he barked and that startled me because he was not a yappy dog. But, when he moved up beside me and fixed his attention on the thermostat, I understood what he was telling me: "Don't touch that dial!" He knew exactly what Dick would have said. I turned to him with my hands on my hips and said, "Don't think you can boss me around. If I want to turn up the heat, that's what I'm going to do. So there." Then I grabbed him and we had a good laugh and also shed a tear or two.

A RIDE I WILL REMEMBER

On a weather-beaten Sunday in mid-February, Brad, my 23-year-old grandson came to take me to his parents' home in Stafford. His mother, Jackie, by far the best cook in the family, and his dad, Jeff, the best griller I know, were preparing a feast to celebrate Jamie and Rob's birthdays. For those who don't know, Jamie and Rob are Brad's sister and brother-in-law.

It seems like only yesterday when Brad, a tiny cherub with rosy cheeks and bouncing blond curls worked his way up from the basement of our split-level home in Dale City. Each time he maneuvered a giant stair with his stubby short legs, he grunted an exclamation. We would never have known what exclamation he chose if his mother hadn't called out, "Brad! Stop saying that!" He had been punctuating each step with "Shit!" a word he'd picked up at his dad's construction site, no doubt.

A short time ago, I watched Brad drive up and park in front of my window and I waved to signal I'd be right out. Before I was half way down the hall, he caught me in a hug. Miss Helena had let him in and she was lingering in the lobby, possibly waiting for a proper introduction. And, of course, she got it. With great pride, I introduced my grandson, Brad, whose stubby little legs had grown long and strong. His hair was cropped so close to his head, no curls could bounce. He towered over us and his engaging smile warmed all corners of the lobby

It was early in the afternoon and the sun was still peeking through the clouds more often than not, but forecasters had predicted a wicked storm for later in the day. Brad's car, a hand-me-down from Jamie's college days, (and Jamie is nine years older than Brad) had already reached 100,000 miles twice, and was well on its way toward a third. Brad readily accepted my offer to have him drive my little Bug.

On the way down to Stafford, Brad talked about his school days. Even though he graduated from high school with honors, he regretted that he'd put so little effort into high school subjects that he had to struggle to keep up during his first two years at George Mason University. He said that by the time he got to his junior year he had much better control over his time. He still had early morning as well as evening swim team practice, but he had learned how to budget time for studying. In the last semester of his senior year and on through the summer he had an internship with the Potomac Nationals (baseball farm team) as groundskeeper. There, he proved he was a dependable worker who could think on his feet. At the end of baseball season, Brad's internship was over and he had no real job - yet.

Half way through dinner, winds began to rage and blow snow sideways. By the time we left, snow had turned to sleet and I would have gripped a dent in the steering wheel but Brad drove as if he drove through sleet every night. He talked about what he had done in the two months after he finished his internship. He sent out resumes and had a few interviews but he didn't sit around and wait for something to happen. He maintained grounds at a business complex and he taught swimming lessons on some evenings. At first he thought he "would not have the patience to work with kids," but found that job rewarding. He remembered problems he'd had in learning certain strokes or lifesaving moves and passed what he'd learned on to his young charges and had the satisfaction of seeing their improvement.

Brad was granted an interview with the Washington Nationals. Yay! He hadn't landed an actual job since it was more like a glorified second internship as a groundskeeper, but in the big leagues. He was thankful for the training he'd had with the local farm team and grateful that his boss at the farm team had set up the interview with the Washington Nationals.

Brad went on to talk about his dad and was especially grateful for the things his dad modeled for him--like his work ethic. Never do a job half way. Get it right and don't complain about how long it takes to do it. Learn to listen to people. Brad also talked about how smart his dad is. His dad never went to college but he could figure out problems in his head as accurately and faster than those who work it out on paper or use a calculator. His dad could look at a picture or an object and build a model from wood. During summers when Brad was in middle school and in high school and not on duty as life guard, he helped his dad on the job. His dad modeled dependability, positive attitude, fairness and skill. I can't recall Brad's exact words, but I got his meaning. By the time Brad had me home, I was glowing inside. Of course I'm proud of Brad, but that dad he was talking about is my very own Jeff.

BLESSED BE THE GLUE THAT BINDS

In our family, customs don't fade away even though life brings changes. Monday night family dinners began more than fifteen years ago, when Donn's daughter, Sara Ashleigh, was in second grade and needed help with reading. I could do that. Monday nights were Donn's night off, so Monday became dinner and reading night. Brother, Mark, learned that Mondays were the best nights to drop in since he could enjoy Donn's company as well as his dad's. Another plus: Monday dinners included dessert. Sara Ashleigh outgrew her need for reading help but Monday nights became established as family dinner nights.

Our family lost three fine men, #3 son, Mark, and then #1 son, Greg, a month later in 2004, and then their dad (my Dick) in 2006. Now, Monday night dinners continue at Westminster. On a Monday night, at the time of this writing. I prepared a simple dinner and was waiting by the window for family to arrive. The first was Donn. I tapped on the window and he looked up, Donn grinned and waved and I was "blown away!" Well, Duh! You expected him, you're probably thinking. Of course, I expected him but the way Donn bounced from his car, shoved the door shut and grinned up at me, showed features and mannerisms exactly like my dad, a grandfather Donn had only seen one time since he was old enough to remember. Donn walks like my dad and he clears his throat before answering a phone the way my dad did. Donn is quiet and easy going, but if pushed too far, the offender had better drop to his knees. My dad was like that.

Donn and his younger sisters, Sara Jane and Caris worked in the Lazy Susan Dinner Theater when they were in high school. Donn was their big brother protector. There, he was known as the Sheriff. If one of the gays came near a sister, the Sheriff appeared. Sara Jane and Caris thought they were quite safe with those gays, but Donn took no chances.

It's no surprise that grandson, Brian, walks like his dad because he's been with him all his life, and I've heard my daughter, Pam, say she was "becoming her mother." But Donn and his grandfather were virtual strangers. How could this happen? The answer must live in their genes, those molecules of heredity that contain a special glue. Blest be the glue that binds.

TAKE CARE OF YOUR MOTHER

Do I believe in spanking? Well, a bit of "force from behind" sends a quick message that behavior is unacceptable. My Scottish grandma told me she kept seven lively offspring in line with switches. She'd send the culprit outdoors to find the proper switch and then apply it to his or her behind. If the switch didn't match the offense, she'd trot that child back out to make a proper selection.

My father and my aunts and uncles turned out great for Grandma, but an assortment of switches was not always available for me, so I used that pancake flipper I have written about. After breaking that instrument of punishment on Greg's buns of steel, I bought a new pancake flipper, and vowed to use it only for the purpose it was designed to accomplish.

Dick occasionally disciplined with a belt. I never saw him apply that belt to the posterior of any of our children, but I've watched him unfasten his belt buckle while looking the offender in the eye until behavior turned appropriate. Then he'd buckle up. I designated a spare belt for my use.

On a Saturday I'll remember forever, Donn, our youngest son, had been out with Deacon Jones collecting money from his paper deliveries and I don't remember what happened to get me so agitated, but since I was irked at Donn, it must have been because he had taken something apart. He had agile fingers that he used to satisfy his curiosity as to how things were put together. Most likely, he had disassembled something I needed and either couldn't get it back together again or hadn't had time to do so. For whatever reason, I stormed downstairs into the family room with belt in hand and confronted Donn. Deacon Jones, who was never a yappy dog, looked from Donn to me and barked loudly, so I ushered Donn into the bathroom, closed the door and gave him a whack. That was the end of that as far as I was concerned, but Deacon Jones on the other side of the door, continued to bark. I was eager to open the door and show Deacon that everything was all right, but Donn said, "Wait, Mom," and stepped out ahead of me just in case his protector had a bite to go with his bark.

I don't know what happened to that belt, but if we'd had a fire blazing in the fireplace, I know I'd have burned that thing down to its buckle.

This scene with Donn when he was nine or ten years old, came back to me clearly in 2006 when I listened to the cell phone message Dick left for Donn moments before he died. His words were, "Donn, take care of your mother."

(Dick, he always has!)

THE CRASH

Don't ever catch your heel in the hem of a pair of slacks you're attempting to remove. I did that once and my descent could not have been more rapid had I slipped on a sheet of ice. I heard something like the sound of sticks clattering on the floor and felt a jolt of pain when my right hip struck the outer edge of the bathtub. I didn't see any of those colorful stars because my head simply sat there in its usual place- untouched. I crumpled to the floor but my glasses remained in place.

I checked out my parts to see what I had that still worked. I had two uninjured arms and a few hours later I got my left leg untangled from my useless right one and found it was intact. Have I told you that floor was cold? I pushed up with my trusty arms but could not stand. I heard my little cat, Tchin, meowing outside the closed bathroom door and I knew he needed me. I'd planned to make an appointment with the vet the next morning. I worried about that little cat because his buddy, a cat he'd lived with for his entire 12 years, had died only weeks before. Now, I was all he had. Get a grip, I told myself; Tchin will be all right.

Okay. I hugged the base of the commode got my uninjured leg and foot to coax down my robe and nightgown from the hook on the door. They became my flimsy blankets and those evil slacks, my pillow. Fortunately, I was still clothed above the waist when I crashed.

I bedded down as much as possible but sleep didn't come. Five light bulbs glared down on me. I had nothing to read except the inch-sized numbers on the clock - a clock that had served our family well when children needed to know the time when they were out in the the pool. They could read that clock from our kitchen window. When I moved from Ashdale to this WLR apartment, my choices were to dump that clock or stick it on the bathroom wall. Thankfully, I stuck it on the wall as it was the only company I had during that long night.

It was slightly after 11:00 p.m. when I crashed and I knew I could last until I was discovered. Since I couldn't push my "Care" button by 9:30 the next morning, I would get a call from the front desk--one I couldn't answer. Kathy Dunn, the nurse in the clinic, would be notified. I wouldn't be on that cold bathroom floor forever. I watched my clock tick off the minutes slowly for the rest of the night and on in to the next morning. At times, I could have sworn the hands stopped moving. At one point, my hope got shaky. The night was so long I began to think the next morning would be Saturday. Kathy wouldn't come on Saturday. Someone would come, but I wanted Kathy Dunn. Finally, my thoughts cleared and I realized it was Thursday night when I fell and Kathy would come for me in the morning.

Shortly after 9:30, my phone rang--the sound I longed to hear. Twice again the phone rang. I listened intently. My bed was still made up from Thursday. What if Kathy saw the made up bed and assumed I'd gone out forgetting to check in? I listened more intently. At last, I heard sounds in my apartment, and called, "I'm in here."

Kathy answered, "Are you all right?"

"No," I replied, and she opened the door. "Oh my God!" she said and then she sprang to action and called to get the EMT's to scoop me up and carry me away. While we waited I got to hold little Tchin and I think he forgave me for neglecting him.

Soon those strong EMTs lifted me off that bathroom floor and onto a stretcher ever so carefully and covered me with blankets. They put me on something very soft in the ambulance and heaped on more blankets. The ambulance driver slowed for every bump. I had spent 11½ hours on that cold floor and that stretcher felt like a heavenly cloud.

Minutes after I arrived at the hospital, Sara Jane, my Occoquan daughter, appeared along with my friend, Marie Polifko. Kathy Dunn had called Sara, but Marie became concerned when I didn't answer her second e-mail. I have no idea how she discovered I was in the hospital that quickly. Then came daughter, Caris, from Arlington and four hours later daughter, Pam, from North Carolina. My loving, caring daughters were bossy -- especially with advice to take pain medicine. They didn't understand that lying on my back with plenty of blankets in a bed after such a close relationship with a hard, cold floor for 11½ hours was all the pain relief I needed. The rest of my family poured in later that day. Sons from Manassas and Stafford, with their families and one son from PA. Greg's widow called from Alaska. All that attention went to prove something I'd suspected for a long time. My kids really do love me in spite of all I put them though.

X-rays showed four breaks in my hip, but prior to the fall my hip was in good shape so it could be repaired rather than replaced. Sounded good to me. The next day, Dr. Hanna inserted 2 titanium rods and told me that if I felt like walking on that leg immediately, I wouldn't mess up his surgery. When I woke up from surgery, my family was there but I wasn't exactly ready to entertain.

After four days, I was released from the hospital and went directly to Westminster's rehab center. Dr. Patel was there. He said. "Remember, this is not a hospital. It's a rehab center," and truer words were never spoken. Therapists got to me before I'd finished breakfast the next morning. I had walked no more than 5 steps in the hospital, but my first morning in Westminster rehab, I walked the length of two halls to get to therapy, did exercises and walked back with a wheelchair following me. Two days later, no wheelchair followed and therapy was tougher. I learned to use a walker, then a cane, and six weeks later, I was done with those devices.

I must say that 43 days from breaking my hip in four places to walking without support speaks well for our rehab center. Also, if I might brag a bit, not bad for an ole lady either.

MY FAITH

My faith is truth I know is present even though I can't prove its existence. It's within me and sometimes comforts me and sometimes disturbs me. My faith is a never failing love that can hold me up and give me hope when tragedy strikes. My faith is a powerful force that directs my thoughts and actions. When I tack the wrong way, it rages within me until I change my course. My faith is trust in an ever-present power, unfailing and superior to any other, and it reveals God's love. My faith is grounded in love of God. God is love.

OUR FAMILY

Above : South Dakota natives with Dick and me in 1984. Below: native South Dakotans celebrating our golden wedding anniversary in 2002. Tim (standing left in back) was dubbed in. He dislikes this photo because the dubber put his arms on backward. For the record: Tim is well put together.

****

Here I am with my 6 SD natives. Mark and Greg died in 2004.

****

Here are some of my grands and greats: back row: Erin, Nick, Brian, Brad and Tommy. Front row: Hannah, Eriah, Jules, Gramma (me), Miccah behind Eric, Sara Ashleigh holding Madalynn, & Jamie holding Carter. October 18, 2013

****

This family gathering at the home of Sara and Chip is helping me celebrate my 90th birthday in 2013. Would you believe there are 20 missing?

****

Thanksgiving in 2007 was our second Thanksgiving without Dad. Back row: Jackie, Charlene, Shanna, Donn, Pam, Dan, Caris, Bill, Brad, Jeff, & Tim. Front" Jamie, David, Me, Erin holding Eriah, Miccah with sun glasses, Nick, Sara holding Eric. And sprawled in front is Tommy with Jules climbing aboard.

We are all thankful for Dad's love, support, wisdom, compassion and gentle but firm guidance. I know he made me a better person and I believe there are others pictured above who will vouch for that.

****

3 of our 4 daughters with their dad:

Left to right: Sara, Dad, Pam, & Caris. Terry, if I had the know-how, I would dub you in.

AFTER I'M GONE

I don't plan on checking out any time in the near future, but since I'm running full steam toward 93 you know I'm a "sprung" rather than a "spring" chicken.

I will tell you how I'd like my memorial service to go, but my friend, Marie reminded me that I would no longer be the one in charge. I realize that you kids are free to do your own thing. Anyway, I hope it bugs your conscience if you don't carry out my plan.

I would like to have my memorial service here at Westminster with members of the Upper Room Sunday School class at St. Paul invited. I want very much to have both Lana Bailey and Marie Polifko in charge of music. If it's feasible for those two special ladies, I'd like to have Marie on the piano and Lana on the organ. If they don't think that will work, how about taking turns on the piano? I most definitely want these pieces: LORD OF THE DANCE and A PLACE IN THE CHOIR with our Kitchen Band Lake Ridge Boys or whatever those men are called at that time, singing A PLACE IN THE CHOIR. Marie and Lana please play any other UP BEAT selections you like. Please **NO HYMNS SUNG BY THE CONGREGATION**!

If any of you kids or grands speak during "Remembrance" time, remember this is a celebration. I want a joyous and fun send off. No mopin'.

I want to be cremated. Absolutely **NO VIEWING.** Divide up my ashes and sprinkle me in the gardens of my children.

One of the many blessings that has made me the happiest is the way our family has stuck together and made us a group of "best friends." Our family gatherings are indeed special and I thank Jeff and Jackie for taking over and hosting these events at Thanksgiving and Easter and Sara and Chip on Christmas Eve when your father and I were no longer able to do so.

I love you.
Mom/Gramma/Betty

Printed in the United States
By Bookmasters